Read and Shoot:

Coaching a Multiple Read Passing Game in the Spread Offense

Dedication

To my beautiful, intelligent, wonderful Lori – thank you for letting me chase my dreams and being the best partner, mother, and wife!

To our children...

> Peyton – gaining you as my daughter made me a better man; can't wait to see where life takes you!

> Austin – more proud of your character than the plays you make, which is saying a ton!

> Grayson – your kind and caring heart is like no one I have ever met...except maybe your Mom!

To our parents – thank you for the example you have set for us and loving us unconditionally.

Acknowledgements

There are so many coaches that have contributed to these pages, as football knowledge is one of tribal understanding -- passed down to the next generation. I need to thank Dennis McWilliams, John Mackovic, and Cleve Bryant for allowing me to step on the field for one of the truly elite programs in college football. Kurt Nichols gave me my first job, where Wes Cope taught me the Run N Shoot offense. Chris Thomsen and Jack Kiser gave me a chance to coach at a truly special place. Phil Wickwar and Tommy Felty let me run their offenses with total autonomy. John Patterson took me under his wing like a big brother and showed me what a great teammate was. Bill Mountjoy shared his enormous football library with me, and the great Homer Smith put up with my incessant questions. And of course, the late John McGregor fed by appetite for football and gained me live access to some of the greatest offensive coaches in pro football.

Specific to this project, I would like to thank Michael Schuttke for editing, as well as Andrew Coverdale and Will Hall for previewing this text. Their opinions mean the world to me, and am very encouraged by their endorsement. Of course, I owe a debt of gratitude to my consulting clients, as they press me to become a better coach, striving for continuous improvement; their teams allow the diagrams in this book come to life.

Lastly, the men who coached with me at St. Mark hold a special place in my heart. Robert Mackey, Mark Helm, Eric Velasquez, and Chris Tenebehn bought in, coached the system verbatim to the best of their ability, and won a championship where it had never been done before. The numbers were truly outstanding, as we averaged a point a minute, completed 71 percent of our passes for 38 touchdowns versus 4 interceptions. Imagine what the stats would have been if they didn't run the clock in seven of our nine games? Best of all, we were all volunteers who coached for the love of our sons. I will never forget our last season at St. Mark.

Read and Shoot:
Coaching a Multiple Read Passing Game in the Spread Offense

Table of Contents

1

Introduction

Introduction

More than half a century ago, Sid Gillman showed the world that one could live via the pass at the pro level. The 70's and 80's then saw the likes of Bill Walsh, Ernie Zampese, Lindy Infante, and Ron Erhardt advance the passing game in the NFL for decades to come. As a college player who played under a former NFL head coach, exposure to an encyclopedic playbook ignited the imagination of this author. Meanwhile, Steve Spurrier innovated the way offense was played in the south, and BYU brought the pro passing game to college football, and (and would spark the mind's eye of the likes of Hal Mumme – Godfather of the Air Raid Offense). Having seen the awesome power of the Houston Cougars' Run and Shoot first-hand as an opposing player, one could only surmise the excitement of learning that passing game from a Jenkins disciple in their first coaching stop. At the second coaching assignment, I was then charged with learning the original BYU offense. After that, I was fortunate enough to have connections that brought me into meeting rooms of Super Bowl-winning coaches, and some of the greatest offenses in pro history. Of equal importance, the late great Homer Smith took the time to correspond with this nobody with a mind full of ideas, and helped make sense of this all. The result, naturally, was a coaching philosophy rooted in the forward pass; moreover, the rare access that I had allowed me to develop a unique vantage point.

Despite the advent of the zone read and the proliferation of the RPO, the drop-back passing game isn't dead. In point of fact, it is quite the opposite. One does not even need to know the number of passing game records that are being demolished; one only needs to look at the increasing standards of performance at football's highest level – the NFL – where the quarterback-driven run game and the RPO are clearly supplementary elements at best. In less than 20 years of evolution, a 60% completion rate went from elite level to mediocre, according to Pro Football Reference. In 1998, the NFL had 7 passers complete sixty percent of their passes; at the same time, there were only three quarterbacks that averaged over 8 yards per attempt. By comparison, through 14 games of the 2018 season, there were THIRTY players completing 60 percent, with 10 passers with over 8 yards an attempt. Perhaps even more telling: the ideas and philosophies of the college game went from being a hindrance to the development of NFL quarterbacks to the backbone of the most successful offenses seen on Sundays. There is an undisputed upward trend in the passing game; however, successful performance isn't limited to teams with big-time college- or professional-caliber athletes. Being a great passing team can happen at any level.

Both as a coach and a father, I place a great deal of credence in being able to teach for the road ahead, and in the belief that learning can occur at any age. So, in 2013, I set out to recreate the passing system I had developed at the college level so that my (then) 8-year old son and his teammates could learn a REAL passing game, rather than what is typically taught at the youth level. The system was a multiple read system that featured quick-rhythm drop back concepts combined the downfield reads of the Run and Shoot with single-back formations and a no-huddle presentation. Fast-forward to 2018 (and now 8th grade), the offense described accounted for 38 TDs/ 4 INTs and a 71% completion rate in 9 games. Whatever verbiage these players need to learn moving forward, the concepts (and most importantly) the "pictures" already present in the player's brain will not change. The ability to process information, track the ball, separate, throw on time, or find space are present and ready for further cultivation – these all create competitive advantage down the road.

This text is not meant to be a playbook; rather, it is an attempt to give insight into teaching and organizational methods that have proven to accelerate the execution of the passing game. My consulting clients have replicated these results across the country at the high school level, resulting in deep playoff runs, record-breaking careers, and state championships. There have been, on multiple occasions, 15-plus percent jumps in completion percentage in the system's first year and all-state performers (one school had 3 different passers named 1st team All-State in 3 consecutive years), but more importantly, the template allows for duplication of passing game success over the years. This should be the goal of every high school program – to have a system that adapts to personnel, yet is rooted in an identity.

2

Read and Shoot: Combining Pro-Style and Spread Principles

Read and Shoot: Combining Pro-Style and Spread Principles

Multiple Formations/ Alignments. With the explosion of up-tempo offenses in high school and college football, there is the observation that many have become so consumed with the idea of running plays as fast as possible, that the actual attacking of the given defense takes a back seat. The elite offenses find a balance between tempo and attacking, but for this reason, there are many ideas that can be gathered from the pros. While it is true that there are many things to be desired from the standpoint of pace, creativity, and even technical teaching at the NFL level, there are also many facets from which coaches learn and develop. When I think of a pro passing game, I conjure very different images in my head than many coaches. Contrary to popular opinion, the system described here is very much a "pro-style" system, as the backbone of this system mirrors the multiple passing games used at the professional level. This interpretation is drastically different than the outdated image that comes to the minds of many – the "pro formation" with two backs, one tight end, and two receivers (Figure 2-1).

Figure 2-1. "Pro" formation

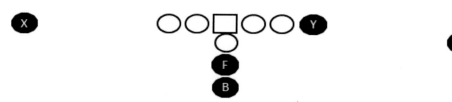

While many football enthusiasts, coaches, and fans may identify the above formation with the term "pro-style offense," further scrutiny reveals that this description is far from fact. In the past ten NFL seasons (2008-2017), there has been a steady decline in the usage of 2-back personnel, with a high of 33% in 2008 (Football Outsiders, 2018). In 2017, the percentage of had dwindled to 12%.

On any given drive, in any given game, an NFL offense will typically align in some type of single back personnel grouping more than 8 out of every 10 plays (Figure 2-2). Clearly, the evidence shows a shift towards offensive football becoming more and more of a "space" game, with little evidence of a swing the other way, especially at lower levels. Because of hyper- focus on the safety aspects of the game (and thus lessening collisions), coaches at lower levels are finding the need to play more within certain constraints, thus inviting more players to participate; clearly, there are benefits of this sort with less crowded LOS players.

Figure 2-2. 1 Back Personnel Groupings by Frequency, 2017.

Personnel	Percentage of total snaps
1 Back, 1 Tight End, 3 Wide Rec.	59.3 %
1 Back, 2 Tight Ends, 2 Wide Rec.	18.8 %
1 Back, 3 Tight Ends	2.8%
1 Back, 4 Wide Receivers	1.2 %
Total	82.1%

One should notice the dependence on the tight end in the NFL; there is a good reason for this. Despite the common spread argument of bringing a defender into the box, the tight end (or H-back) creates adjustment problems for certain defenses (particularly 3- down fronts). Further, the movement of the tight end body, typically the strength indicator for defenses, can create match-up problems for the defense (Figures 2-3 and 2-4), to say nothing of the potential structural problems that can be presented by simply having another gap in the front to fill.

Figure 2-3. If a defense is reluctant to travel their corners, they could become vulnerable to a situation like below – the boundary corner is a force player, almost necessitating the B to stay weak. To the 3-receiver surface, M is in a bind as he is simultaneously responsible for the "B" gap and carrying Y on any vertical release.

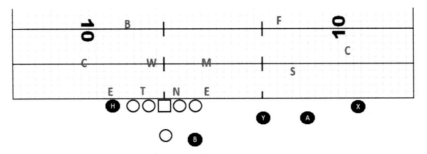

Figure 2-4. Below, this 3-man front must use the 2 outside linebackers as frontal players. As a result of the necessity for R to fill the gap created by the presence of the TE, there is the almost guarantee of strong rotation.

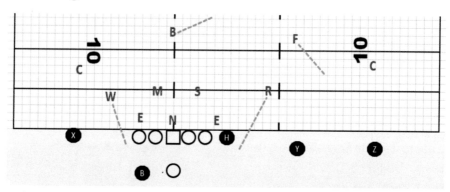

Let the two examples above suffice in displaying challenges that moving the "tight end" (or a tight end body) can give the defense. Because of the flexibility pro teams look for when drafting athletes, it is easy to group single-back personnel groupings together; tight end/H-backs are deployed out wide as much as they are attached to a formation. The idea to note here is that, while few high schools have a Rob Gronkowski or Travis Kelce, most have "tweener" type bodies that can perform the duties of blocking a slot defender giving a larger target for a quarterback on a short route. In many school settings, there is a chance that a tight end or H-back type is a better football player than the fourth wide receiver.

When this author thinks of the term "pro-style" passing game, many thoughts come to mind, and they almost never involve the "I" formation or 2-back, 1-tight end personnel, which was passed as the personnel grouping in the NFL long ago. In addition to single-back personnel groupings, the expansion and contraction of formations, along with the addition of motion to create mismatches, are integral.

It can be also noted that though the term "spread" in describing one's offensive attack, can be seen as generic as one could imagine. Even on the highest levels of college football, though many high school teams are now using four wide receivers, they are usually very static in nature, featuring standard formations with very little split variations from the below (Figure 2-5):

Figure 2-5. Basic 4-Wide Receiver formations.

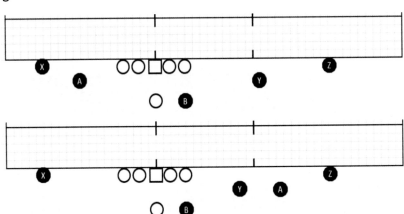

In the above examples, a well-coached defense would expend little effort in aligning, covering, and even pressuring these formations. In fact, the proliferation of the spread offense at all levels means that the above formations are as easy to align to as the I-formation was to standard 8-man front defenses. In response to up-tempo offenses, many defenses have pre-programmed responses based on the offense's formation. These facts are not necessarily bad things, as the astute offensive coach could, in turn, use these automatic checks to his advantage. Here, we give 2 scenarios where the slightest adjustments can alter the defensive plan, thus undressing the defense for the QB.

Below, the "stacked" receivers to the field force a "cloud" (corner force) adjustment in the defense. In order to match any inside vertical threat, the S must widen beyond his normal alignment, and the front side safety (F) must now expand to compensate for the rolled up corner (Figure 2-6):

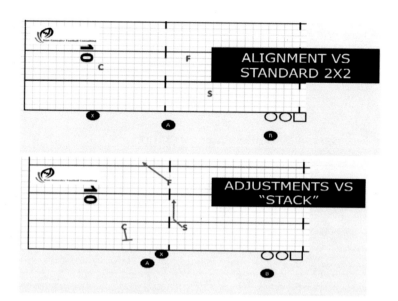

The typical response to a 3x1 set is to have the backside safety (B) cross key to the #3 receiver. With quick motion outside the single receiver, the defense boundary corner, safety, and linebacker must all communicate immediately or be exposed by the offense (Figure 2-7).

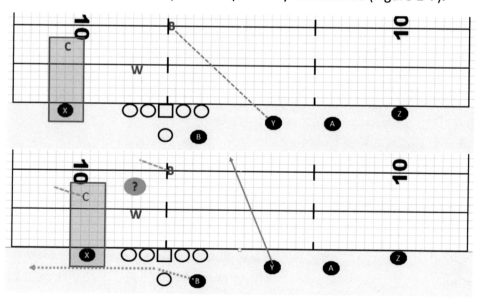

In the above diagram, one can see the conundrum the defense finds itself in with only seconds to communicate. Does the B safety check back to quarters? If so, who will carry the vertical release by Y? If they stay with the call, does W leave the box? In following chapters, this specific scenario will be discussed in regard to specific attack ideas.

Protection Adjustments. With pressure packages becoming more and more prominent as an answer to spread attacks, it also becomes incumbent on an offensive staff to equip the offense with the means to combat blitzes with more than simply "throwing hot" or relying on the screen game. Protection adjustments are necessary that could inhibit many blitz ideas; further, they can be run with just about any personnel grouping. While there are many ideas that can come to mind, the three most common:

- *Re-direct the slide.* In the top drawing (Figure 2.8), the play call features a half man/ half slide protection, with the line sliding to the left and the back check-releasing off of the W. A false cadence (an essential tool in the no-huddle arsenal) reveals movement towards Tampa 2. Because M must cover the deep middle, there is no blitz threat to the called slide side; W is revealed as the only blitz threat. The QB could then simply make a call to slide the line to the right, thus freeing the back to release into the pattern immediately.

Figure 2-8

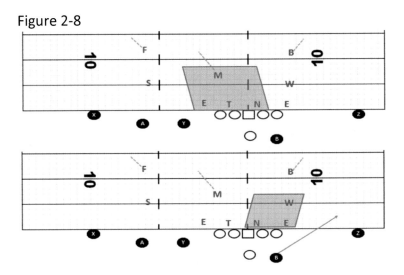

- _Chip protection_. With many offenses giving the defense two open sides, there is a degree of vulnerability to a great edge rush. An often underutilized solution is that of the "chip" block, where the designated helper checks his blitz pickup responsibility, then delivers a blow to the outside half of the designated rusher. Without changing the philosophy of the protection structure, a method for calling and delivering help is critical in the creation of explosive plays in the passing game.

Figure 2-9. Here, a stutter-go route is the goal vs. single coverage. Because of the emphasis of the call, the running back can be assigned to a "slam" route, which is basically what a tight end executes on in a traditional boot/ naked scheme.

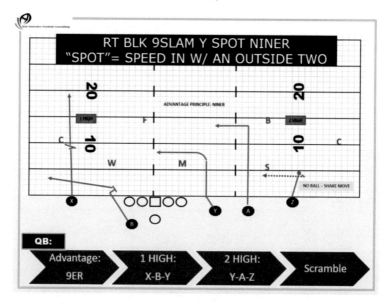

- _Mike protection_. Here, the core offensive line is redirected to have the four down rushers and the middle linebacker, and the running back now checks the outside linebackers from backside to the frontside. With the base protection being of the typical half-man/ half-slide variety, this adjustment can help negate overload blitzes. On the left, the line is sliding for the W, with the back being responsible for the first blitzer inside-out. With M and S rushing, the offense is forced to sight adjust or "throw hot" in order to get the ball thrown before the free rusher arrives. With a simple call at the line, the line is given the M, and the back would now have the two overhang defenders. The offense now has a blocker for every rusher versus the exact same blitz, and is no longer obligated to make a quick throw. The tactic of bringing 4 defenders to a given side no longer means an automatic throw short of the line to gain in a 3rd and Long situation.

Of note here is that protection of the passer is a shared responsibility, and can be accomplished at many different levels within the offensive unit. Along with the three quick examples given here, more insight will be given in regard to game planning and calling the game.

Figure 2-10. "Mike Protection" Audible

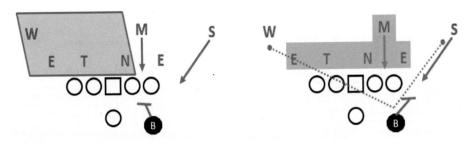

Post-snap route adjustments. As defenses have had to adjust and learn to play against RPO-based passing games, they have had to also become better at not only aligning to formations, but disguising intentions as well. In turn, today's sophisticated passing games must, of course, have the means to adjust to the defense post-snap. Too often, particularly in the RPO era, the defense can dictate where the ball goes. To add to the complication, "checking" to a new pattern at the line is often time consuming, and simply allows the defense to audible after the offense changes the play. The results here could be disastrous (Figure 2-11):

Figure 2-11. Dangers of making all adjustments pre-snap.

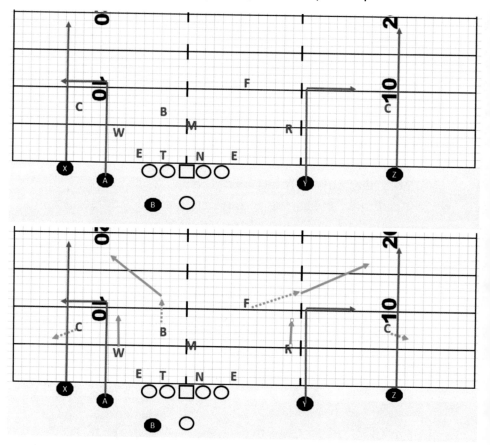

The "look back" tempo procedure has its merit; but if used as the sole method for getting into the right call, there is the natural danger of the defense dictating to the offense. In the above example, there are clear man/ pressure indicators pre snap. But, if the offense regularly audibles, it could simply be to bait the offense into dialing up a man pattern into a Cover 2 disguise. Instead, consider the thoughts provided in Figure 2-12. Here, there is the desired pattern vs man is available; in addition, the seam read on the left is available to beat any type of zone coverage. Most importantly, the ability to direct the passer's thought process is provided within our system.

Figure 2-12. Full-field, multi-purpose pattern.

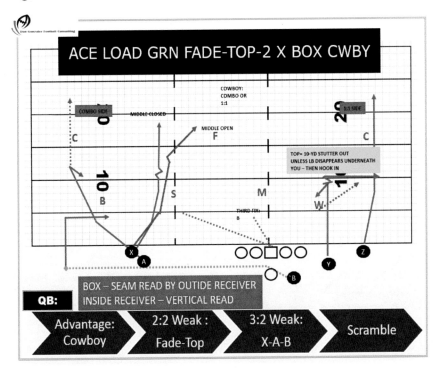

While some routes must be "locked" (i.e. the route is run no matter what, with no conversion based on coverage) to preserve timing, there must be a component that will allow the offense to get the ball to a given player, regardless of coverage – or dictate the consequences to the defense. Using the aforementioned formation and alignment concepts previously described, the offense can gain the leverage it desires (Figure 2-13). In the following illustration, one can see the stack alignment to get a predictable response, then RB motion outside to force a reaction. All the while, the goal is to isolate the offense's best option route runner on an outside linebacker. There are also quick rhythm, locked in routes available in cavities that would be left vulnerable if the defense doesn't adjust properly. But again (and most importantly), there is a method to getting and redirecting (if need be) the passer's eyes to the target to exploit weak points of a given coverage and defensive structure.

Figure 2-13. Isolating Y with an "option" route.

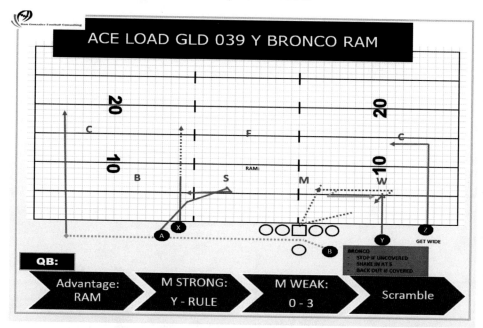

Single back formations with varied player types playing various positions can provide one of the most user-friendly means of diagnosing and attacking a given defense. When combined with solid foundations in the running game and screen package, and mated with the ability to present to the defense in a no-huddle environment, a team will have a superior method of moving the ball.

This author's iteration of what a "pro-style" passing attack involves both pre- and post-snap keys and a reading system that will not allow an offense to counterbalance defensive tactics, but will allow a program to accelerate player development as well. In other words, the packaging of ideas described here has been proven at sub-varsity levels; because more offense can be executed earlier, player execution during varsity competition will be maximized.

3
Building a Learnable System

Building a Learnable System

Knowledge is power – this adage used to be undisputed, whether it was the business world or the coaching ranks. However, the argument can be made that this statement is no longer true. The advancement of technology and availability of information has truly leveled the playing field in terms of the acquisition of knowledge is concerned. Despite this, however, there are those that can achieve sustained success while others toil in mediocrity. The easy answer would be to point at the disparities in talent; however, the same can be said of the National Football League, where talent is abundant everywhere. Further, it is easy to see that most of the systems in the league come from a handful of origins, so the knowledge base is evenly distributed. One needs to look no further than the turnaround of the Rams and their quarterback Jared Goff from the 2016 to 2017 seasons. Clearly, it the coaching application of Sean McVay's version of the West Coast offense that was the deciding factor here.

For those at the high school level, many lessons can be gleaned from these occurrences. At no other level is the development of a program from top to bottom so important, and at no other level is teaching so critical. And while history has shown that trends in football have been cyclical, the current state of the game represents a new age. With player safety issues looming over the sport, not to mention the state of societal preferences in general, there is a high degree of probability that changes back towards a "ground and pound" era from tight formations are unlikely. Teams will always want to be able to control the ball on the ground, though most likely using spread principles or perimeter adjustments to counter front and pressure trends on the defensive side. These factors are all to be weighed in designing an offensive system, and the one presented here represents a means blend all of the elements described, while expanding the ability to be learned by younger players.

When talking with coaches, the question arises in regard to "must have" elements; often, they are asking about specific plays. Rather than covering individual pass patterns, it is found that it is best to have principles that must be adhered to. In the previous publication, Recoded and Reloaded, the following musts were identified and detailed:

- Give receivers the opportunity to defeat tight man coverage.
- Prevent conflict between receivers.
- Have a defined timing.
- Stretch the defense vertically and horizontally.
- Keep the QB out of interception danger with the movement of his eyes.
- Deny pattern reading by the defense.
- Minimize one-for-one trades.
- Keep receivers from free pass defenders.
- Have a principle of route conversion.
- Adjust to condensed field areas.
- Have the ability to isolate certain parts of a pass defense.
- Allow for quick throws when the defense is outflanked.
- Accommodate delays and screens.
- Have set reading concepts.
- Have organized scramble rules.
- Have the ability to adjust to multiple formations.

It is easy to see how the bullet points can enhance many of today's passing games would benefit from these principles.   Even at the highest levels of college football, it has been observed that far too many offenses have centered their passing games on the RPO, without a foundation for an intermediate passing attack capable of sustaining possession of the ball. The result here would be a highly disjointed attack, relying on RPOs and "go" routes to sustain an attack. Without a high percentage intermediate game, the offense is unable to fully dictate to the defense, and thus left hoping to connect on 50/50 deep balls when the defense clamps down on the RPO. In order to keep the offense "playing downhill," the following are highly recommended:

Make the defense be truly "plus one" when throwing hot. In an attempt to reduce 1-on-1 protection responsibilities, some coaches simply gave the QB a single linebacker to throw "hot" off of (Figure 3-1).

Figure 3-1. Defensive trap if QB is forced to throw hot vs single blitzer.

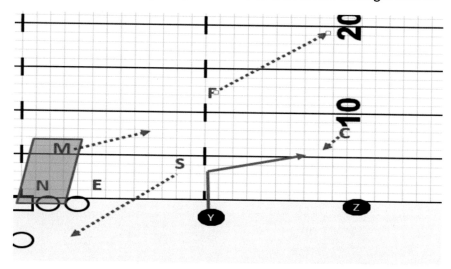

The problem is that the defense always has an extra player; the result is that the defense can "trap" the hot throw whenever they want. The rules of the protection should always ensure that the passer only makes a "hot" throw when rushers truly outnumber the protectors on a side (Figure 3-2). The offense can also limit "4 to a side" blitz opportunities for the defense in careful use of formations/ alignments (Figure 3-3). In Figure 3.2, the slide has the line sorting for any three rushers, forcing an unblocked rusher to come from the outside.

Figure 3.2. Protection rules requiring 4 man side to trigger "hot."

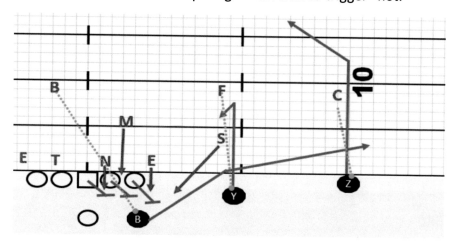

Figure 3.3. Discouraging 4 man blitz. QB and X responsible for W

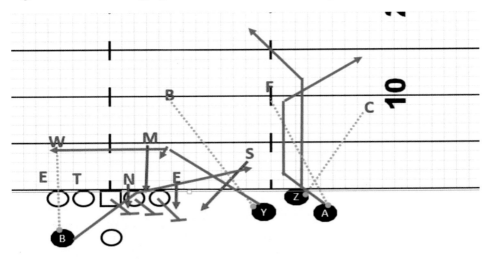

All Eleven Players are involved in the Protection Unit. Protection is not limited to the offensive line and the quarterback. In addition, it is preferred that the pattern structures on the hot side have multiple built-in quick breakers to serve the passer. It is important to note that these quick throws must have a vertical component. To do so, the theme of rhythm must be built in to every component of teaching. For example, in the pattern here, the flag route by Y breaks at 6 steps, with an aiming point of 20 yards. This provides a sharp contrast to the teaching of many, which is as a 12-yard route with a varying landmark based on coverage. As a result, the route can be available in a rhythm drop, and the ball can be released immediately because of the definitive angle. Furthermore, the accompanying route stems are designed to give the quarterback a clearer picture at the snap than with traditionally taught combinations (Figure 3-4). The angled release by the outside receiver forces a man coverage defender to chase, giving the passer a clear indicator at the snap of the ball. With this key present at the snap, the decision is triggered earlier than in the traditional combination in Figure 3-5.

Coupled with the faster route stem and fixed landmark, these elements provide a quick rhythm, downfield option vs pressure.

Figure 3-4. Speeding up recognition for the throwing the corner route.

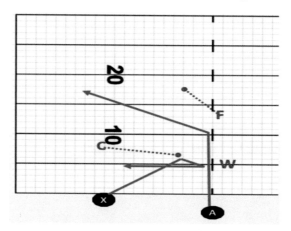

In contrast (Figure 3-5), one can see the traditional "Smash" combination with a wide hitch and flag route. Versus a soft man technique, the corner can still retreat, giving the QB no indication that the flag should be thrown. Two things will happen in this instance: first, the corner will be driving on the hitch while ball is in the air. Second, the opportunity given by the defense for an explosive play will be missed. And because the ball will be held longer by the

Figure 3.5. Traditional route stems on the "Smash" combination

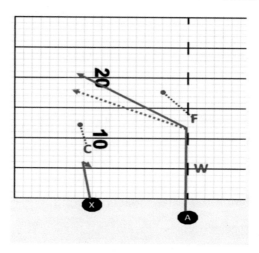

Play with multiple tempos. The ability to run the offense at a rapid pace is enhanced with the ability to change tempos, as it forces the defense to declare its intentions. If defenders are wary of the ball being snapped quickly, they must get into their final alignment; stemming and coverage disguise can be minimized, allowing for the offense to dictate. While no disguise is completely avoidable, defenders will find themselves out of position and vulnerable to a well-designed attack. Having established a baseline tempo, the opportunity to check out of bad plays will present itself. This is where a "lookback" or "check with me" tempo will prove to be extremely effective, as it will allow an offense to stay on schedule and generate more explosives. Even greater than reducing negative plays, perhaps the greatest benefit of multiple tempos to the offense lies in the ability to practice more efficiently (Figure 3-6), as plays can now be paired with companion plays that will create a solution to problem defenses. Players will then know the strengths and weaknesses in their own offense, and learning will be at its highest level.

Figure 3-6. Counter Read and paired blocking adjustment.

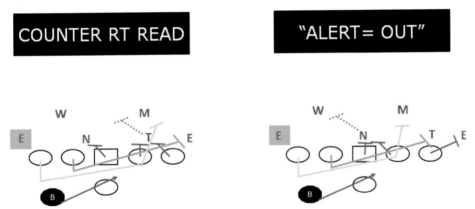

No longer do players have to learn to execute every play vs. every look; in the diagram above, the counter play is paired with an adjustment when confronted with a "50" look. Because of the pairing, referred to as an "Alert" in this offense, the entire unit knows the possibilities. Further, each adjustment can be practiced solely versus that specific look, enhancing efficiency be avoiding wasted practice repetitions.

The blending of tempo combinations is something that is available, yet seldom used. From the chart below (Figure 3-7), a majority of teams at the high school level have an equivalent pace; however, the observation can be made that an opponent can predict a majority of the situations where the corresponding tempo will be used.

Figure 3-7. Tempo chart.

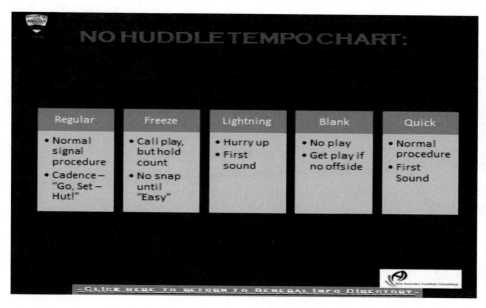

If a defense can be made to guess, however, the usage of different play call rhythms can be a major propellant of an offense's success. Game planning packages can then be built more effectively by having sustainable elements over the course of the season, and not just versus specific opponents.

Use the back as a multiple pass threat. One of most critical matchups in the passing game can be found between the running back and the linebackers. All too often, these (often favorable matchups) are neglected by the design or calling of the offense. However, because of the advancements in the spread offense in general, coverage theory has had to evolve in order to build brackets and help defenders from being isolated downfield. Figure 3-8 illustrates a coverage that has grown in popularity to 3x1 sets; with the FS poised to help strong with a vertical

28

release by Y and M pushing strong to match with the 3rd man to the strength, B can easily be isolated on the W.

Figure 3-8. Split-field coverage.

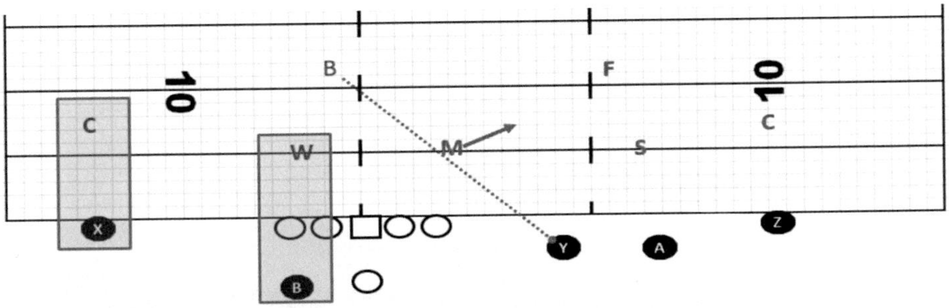

Many offenses relegate their running back (labeled "B" in these diagrams) to screens or check-down passes. However, against the coverage above, one of the most explosive routes that could be featured is a "read" or "option" routed to the running back, allowing him to simply defeat the leverage of the isolated linebacker by crossing his face. The way that patterns are built in this system ensures the read is only thrown in a 1 on 1 isolation; much like the "Alert" example in the running game, coaches should strive to ensure maximize the efficiency of the pattern by programming a specific picture for the offense, teeing it up, and letting the offense execute.

While surface inspection would have many questioning the ability to teach specialized routes to this position group, one should recognize that running backs are typically among the most gifted athletes on the offensive team. Teaching the finer points of these routes can be done in conjunction with receiver groups. Detractors may say that a "Marshall Faulk-type" is necessary to execute some of the detached pass routes in this system; it has however been proven that the matchups are relative, and certain patterns can open up more of themselves simply by forcing the defense into an unfamiliar structure. Figure 3-10 demonstrates how this system's terminology allows the back to fit into different areas of a pass pattern, without memorization.

Figure 3-9. B Bronco to isolate W Linebacker.

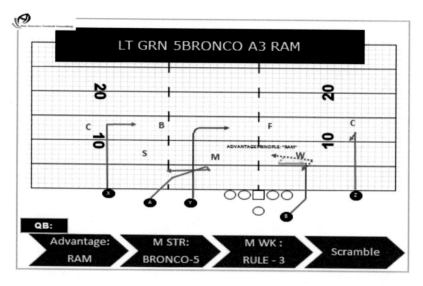

Figure 3-10. A variety of routes with no memorization. B's routes are highlighted in green.

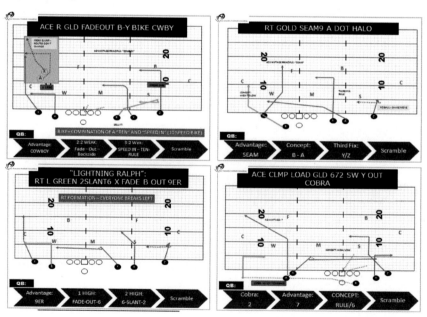

If anyone can master the demands of running certain cuts, the most skilled athletes in a high school program can. In addition, this is exactly what some pressure schemes are counting on eliminating from the offense. Many times, there is poor accounting for the running back in certain pressure schemes; Figure 3-11 is a prime example of this.

Figure 3-11.

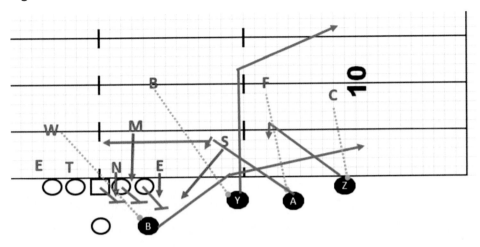

While many instances discussed involve a free release of the back, there must also be the means to avoid the hot throw. Protection schemes must also support this goal. Figure 3-12 demonstrates a protection scheme in the offense that free releases the B, without introducing anything new for the offensive line.

Figure 3-12. Tar/Teal Protection= Half man/ half slide with H/TE as the check releaser.

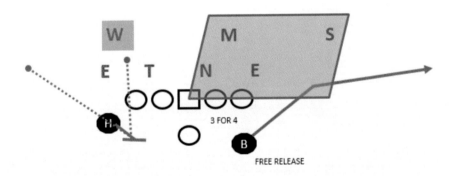

Allow for learning to let players play fast. With the advent of tempo-based attacks, many are aware of snapping the ball at a rapid pace. However, in the process, many have watered down their attacks because the systems involved little more than rote memorization. The result here is either an inordinate mental burden placed on the player, or an offense that MUST rely on simplicity in order to sustain itself. Who, in their right mind, would actually choose fewer options at one's disposal? The answer is no one; some simply don't have the apparatus to have variety.

Simplicity is not based on having a short play call. Take the example in the following diagram (Figure 3-13). A word system might have a name like SPOT to denote the structure – in this system's verbiage it's called 471. In a very static environment, there are no issues; however, once there is the desire to change elements of the pattern (perhaps due to the dictation of the defense), complications become apparent. For example, to move a player within the formation, he would, in effect need to learn multiple positions.

Figure 3-13. Comparing Naming Conventions and Learning.

Naming convention	Play name	Backside Combination	From 3x1	Move Z to run corner	Change backside	Change QB Read
Words	SPOT	Memorized	New Learning	New Learning	New learning	? Sideline conversation
Numbers	471 X2	Tagged (X2)	Digits indicate	Change digits (741)	Tag indicates	Tag Indicates

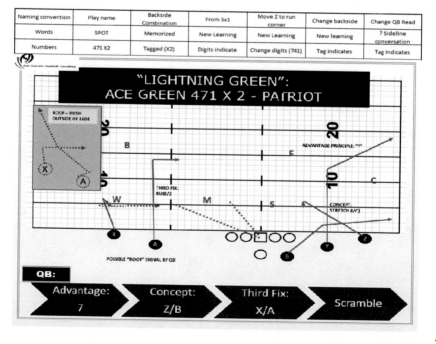

As one can imagine, as variations get further from the base, more and more learning is required of not only the person we want to move, but by extension, by all other receivers as well. On the other hand, in this system's choice of verbiage, players simply listen to their spot in the play call chain. With the play call speaking to each individual player, learning burden is lifted, thus ensuring maximum speed in execution. Even with very young players, or first year players in the system, missed assignments are non-existent with this method. Teaching can then focus on the finer points of teaching, such as technique and adjustments versus different defenses; the coach is granted full flexibility without inordinate time being spent on teaching assignments. As further illustration of this point, refer to the following table (Figure 3-14).

Figure 3-14. Sample grid

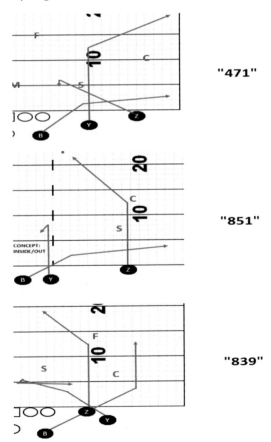

"471"

"851"

"839"

33

If the reader is asked to concentrate on the first digit in each line (if the call side is toward him), for example, it is easy to see how the confusion on the part of the player can be avoided. The result is that players can not only play faster in terms of freedom from hesitation is concerned, but can reach the field at an earlier stage as well. A talented underclassman is now able to contribute immediately. For a coaching staff, this means that the talent available to be utilized to its full potential in the deployment of the offense.

Are there one-word calls in this system? Certainly. However, the defense can be attacked with a full spectrum of weapons, without an inordinate amount of rote memorization, and without watering down the overall offense with this method. Best of all, this array of tools is at the disposal of the quarterback, who can be guided by the coach as closely or as freely as necessary.

Provide the platform for moving star players. As an extension of the previous thought, the age of advanced defensive tactics make it more critical than ever to be able to move special players within the formation. No longer can an offense count on isolating a great outside receiver, because an astute defensive staff simply will not allow an offense to do that to them.

Figure 3-15. Methods for doubling X in 3x1 sets.

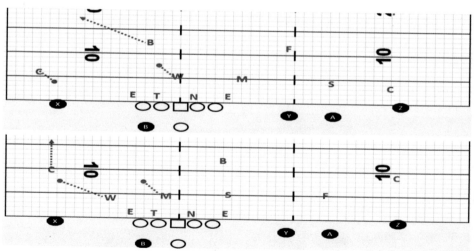

Of course, an offense can "take what the defense gives," but the ever-present fact of offensive football is that explosive plays must be created. The most obvious example involves the classic "X" receiver in most offenses (Figure 3-15). Though there is plenty of opportunity in standard 2-2 sets, defenses are too well designed to leave an overmatched corner in an isolated situation.

Most teams could not afford to neglect their very best playmakers, and this author's team was no exception. So, players had to be moved in the formation at times. Figures 3-16 through 3-19 show just a few places where the X receiver was aligned in order to avoid double teams and maximize potential explosives.

Figure 3-16. X in stack with B motion outside.

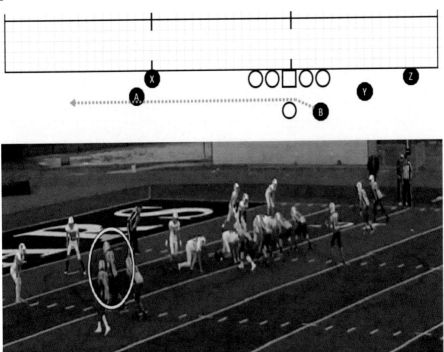

Figure 3-17. X is the point man in "Bunch"

Figure 3-18. X is #2; Y and A exchange sides in "Ace" formation.

Figure 3-19. X is #3 to in a 3 man surface. B forms weak stack.

For further evidence that this is something that is sustainable, it should be noted that the still shots that accompany each diagram involve middle school players that practiced twice per week.

Have overlap in attacking coverages. In meeting with coaches across the country, perhaps the most common question is "what do you like?" in regard to passes versus a given coverage. The answer from this coach's point of view is always complex; there are so many variables to each coverage, and complex rules to deal with variations within that coverage.. It has been proven much more effective to develop patterns, reading principles, and coaching points that defeat techniques within the coverage. From there, we simply package elements to put defenders in a bind. Figures 3-20 through 3-22 demonstrate this way of thinking.

Figure 3-20. Pass to defeat multiple coverage categories.

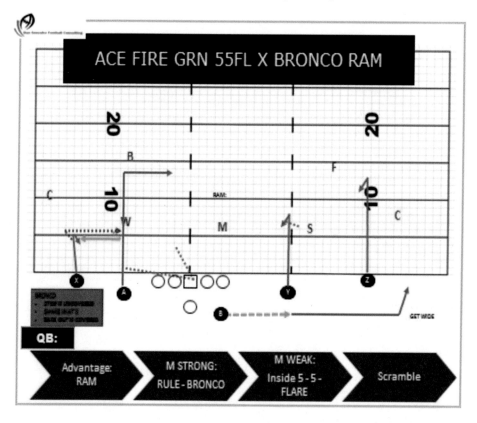

Here, the A is given the direction that he must achieve his depth and must cross the backside safety's (B) face. X is told to run a width stop, all the while with his eyes on the defender inside of him (W), and is given instruction on how to react to him to either uncover or pull him out of the lane. The quarterback is directed to dissect the underneath coverage by working opposite the Mike, and work inside-out to whatever side that turns out to be, as the result should be a "plus 1" situation in favor of the offense to that side. The idea of working away from the drop of the middle linebacker is nothing new, as it was the thought used in the popular "all curl" pattern, although there is a difference here in the variety of defenses the pattern could defeat.

Figure 3-21. Mike goes weak

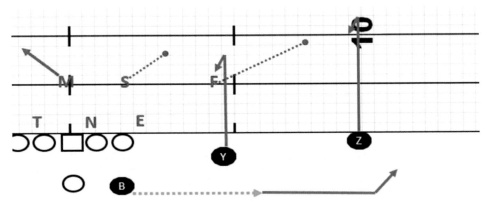

When the Mike, identified as the 2nd LB to the 2 releaser surface, goes weak (Figure 3-21), there is a strong possibility of 4-under, 3 deep coverage. If this is the case, the three receivers to the strong side outnumber the two underneath zone defenders, and a completion should be readily available. Should Mike rotate to the field, the W will be stretched by the A and X receivers (Figure 3-22). The adjustments in X's route will allow for the most space available, and, again, a completion will be likely.

Figure 3-22. Isolation on W with M rotating to field.

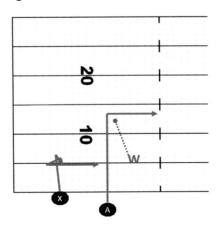
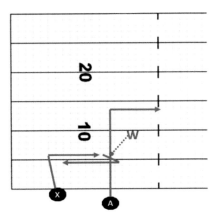

The idea here is to eliminate as much identification as possible; once again, this is to allow players to "play fast." One should not paralyze a player by forcing him to identify the exact coverage, as there are simply too many variables.   It is the belief here that players can be given instruction based on the actions of adjacent defenders, but that expecting one to know the entire defensive stricture is not realistic, and not necessary.

4

A Method for Teaching

A Method for Teaching

In this age of information, in which the advancements of the greatest minds in the history of the game are available to the masses, there is truly wonderful theory in abundance. Where there is disconnect, however, is whether or not the theory can be put into practice and executed under the pressure of winning and losing. There are situations where even poor teaching is successful because of the talent of the athletes or the situation of the program (ex. Great resources, numbers, or intellectually advantaged students). More often, however, coaches have fallen back on the K.I.S.S. method in their teaching. While there is nothing at the root of this sentiment, further scrutiny can argue that the result of this teaching will often result in average results. This system balances the two trains of thought, as it maximizes the volume of offense at the disposal of the staff, while minimizing the assignment burden of the line, backs and receivers. Most of all, it gives the quarterback guidance with baseline principles, and maximizes situational execution by allowing the coach to override default instruction and give specific, purposeful—and previously practiced—redirection on any given play.

It has been stated on many occasions that this system is an attempt to simplify the very complicated. With a myriad of pattern possibilities to go against the advances made in modern pass defenses, it is the strong opinion of this author that the way to start is by making sure individual learners have zero hesitation when the play call comes in from the sideline. The passing game can be likened to many forms of complex ideas, whether that be a business plan, or military strategy. In conveying any sort of complex information, it is to be noted that the information is never about the presenter (the coach), but rather, always about the audience (the players). After decades of studying both play calling systems and learning styles, it was decided that the resulting system provided the best results in terms of not only assimilation, but retention as well.

What's in a name? Words vs. Numbers

Many ponder this question in regards to play-call nomenclature. While some may say that "kids aren't good with numbers," they are often referring to the fact that many people (this author included) don't enjoy math. However, if asked to put numbers into order, or create equivalent associations (such as with dominoes or dice), people would rarely have difficulty. Likewise, in assigning a number (from 0-9) to an individual route, and translating a numbered combination into a pass pattern, a player would have no difficulty.

After examining learning numerous models, a formula for calling pass plays was developed that could support any pattern, adjustment, and (most importantly) read concept. Study has shown that as long as rules could be provided, such as in the play call chain (Figure 4-1), a much broader number of combinations could be learned than with other methods.

Figure 4-1. The play call chain

43

In fairness, many teams operate using words to identify pass patterns. For an "apples to apples" comparison, one should exclude professional teams in this regard, as unlimited time and a higher level of expectation is involved. In other words, while X's and O's in the NFL may be superior, the teaching methods may not be. When using words for concepts, it is important to note that when speaking of a handful of plays being used, the naming convention does not matter. When built on a proper base, there is a negligible difference. However, if one is to use multiple variations, then the numbering system used here has a distinctive advantage, as the individual player simply listens for their spot in the chain in this numbering system.

The protection, denoted by a color, also represents the front-side of the pattern. An R or L in the color denotes this directional indicator (Figure 4-2):

Scheme	Frontside Left	Frontside Right	Learning Cue
5-Man Dropback	Gold	Green	"G" tells RB he is GONE
6-Man Dropback	Black	Brown	"B" tells RB 1st Responsibility is Blitz Pickup
6-Man w TE	Teal	Tar	"T" - TE is check releaser; Line slides TO call
Max Dropback	Metal	Maroon	"M" means MAX. Full time blocker

At the high school level, it is possible to have one scheme (half man, half slide) account for all of the above as a base. Further, from the standpoint of teaching, this is desirable, as the basic protection principles do not have to change for junior varsity, freshmen, or even middle school levels. With a distinctive base, it is ensured that all repetitions are meaningful and that proper building can occur.

In the direction of the call, receivers listen to the digits, and run the corresponding number of a route tree (Figure 4-3), from the outside-in. There is very little variation between the inside and outside assignments, thus meaning there is very little nuance, once again making for better teaching.

Figure 4-3. Route tree summary.

#	Descriptuon	Inside Rec Adjustment	Outside Rec Adjustment
0	Locked Seam		
1	Flat	Stop	
2	Under	Stop, then under	5 yard in
3	Pivot (Fake Drag)		
4	Spacing Hook		
5	Turn	Curl	Stick
6	Move Drag		
7	Flag		
8	Post		
9	Outside Vertical	Stutter Go	Wheel
TEN	Trail (Fake Flat)		

The outside receivers (X and Z) always listen for the first digit, the slots (A and Y) are alert for the second number, while the back listens for the last. From this basic starting point, there are only a handful of tweaks, mainly dealing with going from a 2- to 3-man surface. Figures 4-4 and 4-5 illustrate these situations. In both cases, the running back has an overriding tag (by having the suffix "B" denote the new route) that tells him he no longer has the last digit in the call – this feature is no different than the tagging procedure in most systems.

Away from the call side, receivers have a simple rule that only has one exception: either run any tagged route (ex. A Out, X 2) or run a "rule" route, which is simply a 12-14 yard IN route. It is called a "rule" because that is the backside rule for patterns; Figure 4-6 shows the basic "Rule" tag, along with its companion, "Switch". Inside-breaking routes are a major part of any full-field attack, and this is how they are introduced as a basic component. Concepts that are integral to the passing game, from maintaining vertical and horizontal spacing to separation techniques at the breakpoint, can all be emphasized with the most elementary backside tags. This way, important methodology can be introduced, and the foundation for teaching more advanced ideas can be placed at the proper stage of development. At the onset of teaching, however, players are taught to run RULE without being told; the lone exception to this structure occurs when there is a SEAM READ in the pattern call. This is a special point of emphasis during installation, and is one of the primary coaching points that is unpacked and emphasized when the offense is being introduced to new learners.

Figure 4-4. Motion from 2x2 to 3x1 = motion man assumes last digit

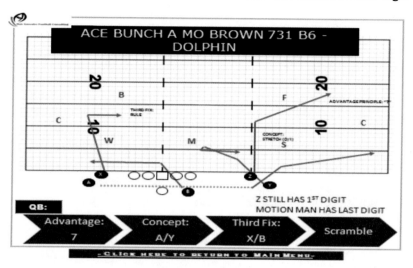

By introducing all rules at the onset, learning is absorbed earlier in the process, and considered "old hat" before the end of the installation process. These findings held true, even at younger levels.

Figure 4-5. Call to strength of a "Trips" formation utilizing a B tag.

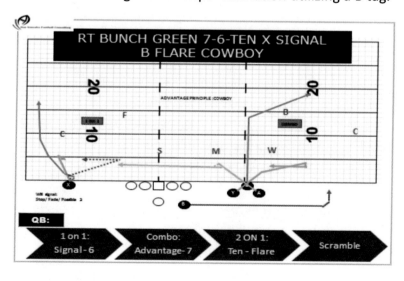

Figure 4-6. "Rule" and "Switch" backside tags

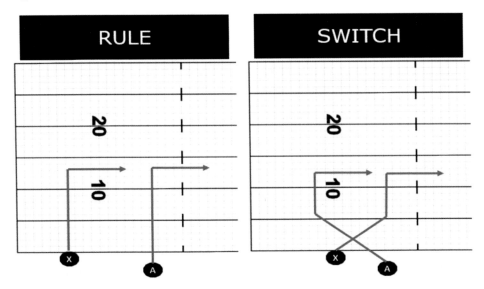

In the instance in which the RB is desired to be a part of the backside combination, the play call would simply have an "R" designation rather than using the letter "B." Using the letter "R" tells the back to go to the "reverse" side (Figure 4-7).

Figure 4-7. "R" tag to send the back away from the front-side.

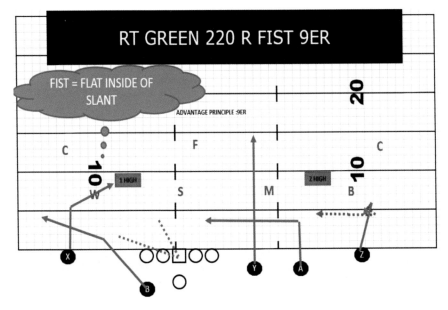

This feature provides two important structural components. First, it allows the back to participate in combinations away from the initial movement of the passer's eyes. Second, and perhaps most importantly, it allows for the back to release to the same side as the slide of the line. Because of the propensity for defenses to base pressure schemes based on the alignment of the back, the importance of this feature cannot be overstated, as this provides an important exception to any keys the defense may use in devising a pressure plan.

With an exception of the above situations, the running back is simply alert for any alignment or motion cues in the play call and runs the last digit. In the diagram below (Figure 4-8), one sees that the motion call takes the back away from the call side, yet does not change the spot in play call chain that pertains to his assignment. This feature, once again, allows a gifted athlete to play fast, as there is no interpretation necessary once the play call is received.

Figure 4-8. Back's assignment denoted in last digit, regardless of motion.

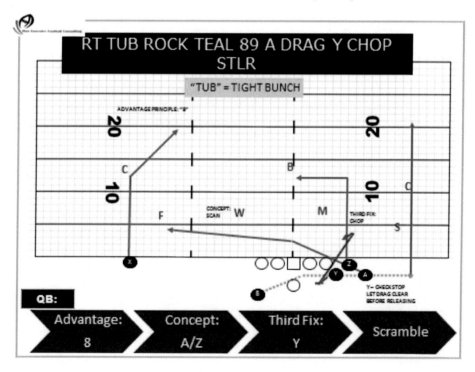

It is easy to see how quickly players can become accustomed to the formula of the play call. Using the examples given, one could further see the depth of variety that can be executed in a relatively simple fashion. As long as a player can rely on one part of the call (the first digit or the last digit), assignments can be carried out without hesitation. The processing here for the player is significantly less burdensome than in having to determine if a worded play call (i.e. "Smash") is being run from a 2x2 or 3x1 formations, and then where the player is within the formation. So, the play call might be simple for the coach, but not necessarily the player.

There are some routes that are named, rather than part of a numbered tree. The name would simply be inserted at the same point of the number, and the player would simply execute the route called in that "link" in the play call chain (Figure 4-9 and 4-10). Once again, as the foundation for learning is set, multiplicity is gained with little new learning; named routes are typically derived from the base, and techniques are already familiar. Take, for example, the "Choice" route, which is a vertical read closely resembling the receiver outside of a seam read (further detail will be revealed in later sections).

Figure 4-9. "Choice" route to frontside combination.

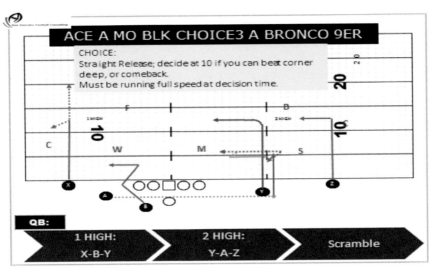

Above, the X receiver is listening for the first term; "Choice" simply replaces a digit in the call. Below, the B is listening for the last digit and executes a "Bronco," which is an option route to be thrown on an isolation vs. the W linebacker.

Figure 4-10. Named route (Bronco) in play call chain.

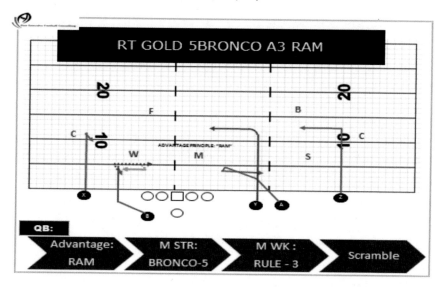

It should be noted that all the combinations in this system have a word-based equivalent (Figure 4-11). If a word-based pattern system is used, it is recommended that some mnemonic theme be used if the base of the passing game is a broad one.

Figure 4-11. Example of named routes using mnemonic terms.

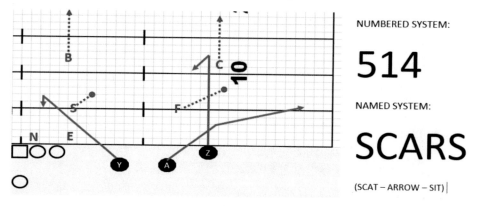

Once again, if there are to be just a handful of patterns in an entire passing game, then any naming system will do. However, if there is to be an amount of breadth to the possibilities, it is recommended that learning be accented not only in the manner in which patterns are called (for the sake of the skill players), but also in the way that they are grouped for the quarterback as well, which is certainly the case here.

Verbiage and Tempo: Can they coexist?

This author has never had a problem with longer play calls; in the case with the numeric system described here, it is apparent that individual skill players are relieved of inordinate amounts of memorization, allowing them to play faster. Moreover, it allows coaches to not be shackled by the fear of missed assignments, instead spending time on technique and opponent study. To downplay such a method while claiming ineffective learning is simply irresponsible, as facts support the assertions made here.

Where there is a legitimate query, however, is regarding the question of tempo, as it stands to reason that signal time is of the essence in the no-huddle world. There are multiple methods that can be examined; it is important to note that over a 5 year period, teams using this system averaged over 65 plays per game at the varsity level. Perhaps more indicative of the effectiveness to which offense was generated lies in the fact that these sample sizes include teams that have driven deep into their state playoff brackets, meaning that many fourth quarters were not spent in "catch up" mode. In other words, maximizing the number of plays ran was not a problem. Depending on the team, one of two primary methods of communication were used: the wristband system or the signal system. There are subtleties to both that allow for no-huddle offenses to have "quick, efficient business meetings" in between snaps.

In the wristband system, each skill player wears a 3-window band that lists all of the plays (Figure 4-12). Each line contains only the play, so that certain formations and/or personnel calls can be adjusted as part of the game plan. There is further organization for the coach, as the left side of the band organizes calls to be made from the left hash mark, while the right side obviously represents calls for the right hash. The play call procedure is very straight forward: skill players receive a base personnel group/formation (as one can see, formation adjustments are on the card) and a number, while the line obtains the blocking scheme.

Figure 4-12. Wristband Example

73	LD GLD 09 Y DOT MAV (ALRT MTL 7)	91	RK GRN 09 Y DOT MAV (ALRT MRN 7)
74	GRN 7-6-TEN X SIG B FL CWBY	92	GLD 2-SWIRL-DRAG B O Z SAIL PAT
75	BRN 467 X8 B1 9ER	93	BLK 467 Z8 B1 9ER
76	BLK 56 A BMER GTR (ALRT AZ RULE)	94	BRN 56 A BMER GTR (ALRT AX RULE)
77	BRN 508 B-3 X SAIL CWBY	95	BLACK 508 B-3 Z SAIL CWBY
78	GLD SEAM9 A DOT HALO	96	GRN SEAM9 A DOT HALO
79	LD GLD 76 A BEAMER COWBOY	97	RK GRN 76 X BOXER COWBOY
80	BRN RULE-3-8 X CHOICE B6 9ER	98	BLK RULE-3-8 Z CHOICE B6 9ER
81	GOLD 5BRONCO A3 RAM	99	GREEN 5BRONCO A3 RAM
82	BLK 61 Y BNGL A-8 MAV	100	BRN 61 Y BNGL A-8 MAV
83	LD GLD OUT-9 A3 MAV	101	RK GRN OUT-9 A3 MAV
84	R GRN 228 B6 X SIGNAL CWBY	102	L GLD 228 B6 Z SIGNAL CWBY
85	RED SEAL LT ALL STOP (ALRT RKT)	103	BLUE SEAL RT ALL STOP (ALRT LSR)
86	A FIRE RED SPLIT LT RD A FLARE	104	A FLAME BLUE SPLIT RT RD A FLARE
87	SWEEP RT (ALRT: NOW)	105	SWEEP LT (ALRT: NOW)
88	CK - BL QB SWP LT CRK Z NOW	106	CK- RED QB SWP RT CRK X NOW
89	STRAW 591 X BENGAL HALO	107	SLATE 591 Z BENGAL HALO
90	BLK 9SLAM Y SPOT 9ER	108	BRN 9SLAM Y SPOT 9ER

For example, with the ball located on the left hash mark, the play caller could simply call for "RIGHT 85." Using the above card, the offense would align in a 3x1 formation to the right (Figure 4-13), featuring play number 85 – signifying the following RPO (Run Pass Option):

Figure 4-13. Diagram of play number 85 on the wristband.

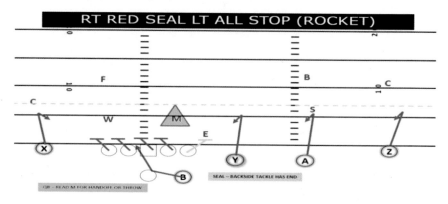

"Seal Left" is a variant of the split-zone run to the left in which the backside tackle locks on the backside end. "All Stop" is obviously the quick game pattern. The explicit play call on the card comes with the adjustment "Alert: Rocket" – which is a crack screen to be run only vs. man to man coverage. Learned as a packaged play, with a reminder in the play call, the QB is equipped to make a check at the line (Figure 4-14) by simply calling "ALERT! ALERT!"

Figure 4-14. Rocket adjustment vs. Man

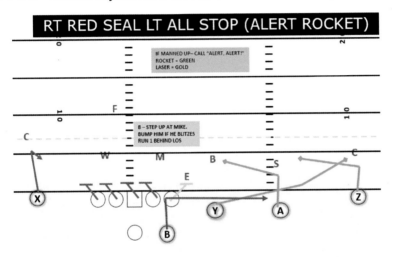

One of the keys to this form of communication is that the offensive line would have a dedicated signal containing only the blocking scheme or protection; the signal they would receive in this case would simply be "SEAL LEFT." This way, they can immediately turn and begin making calls as the receivers move to position. In terms of a timeline, this is much faster from call to snap than many communication systems that rely on the QB getting the signal, then relaying the play, then beginning the cadence. Using this method, an expansive menu is available without a question in terms of assignment, and signaling is kept to a minimum. Further, every play has the same number of signals -- Runs, RPOs, Play Action, Dropback – all without a tipoff to the defense.

And while many may dislike the idea of generating new cards, it should be noted that the attention and care to the necessary components drives the installation process, ensuring minimal change. During the 2018 season, the need for wristband changes from summer through the playoffs happened exactly two times. Moreover, the wristband worksheet ties into the practice scripts and game plan – once again driving an efficient offensive process. Using basic software codes, spreadsheets can be useful time-saving tools; more detail will be visited in the game planning section of this text.

For those that are absolutely resistant to wristbands, communication systems involving multiple signalers provide an efficient means to convey the information. For those with small coaching staffs, backup players are excellent options. There are many configurations that could function effectively; the key to the signal system is to break up the transmission. Ideas include: signal by position group, signaling to the left side vs the right side, or dividing by frontside/ backside. Of course, the ability to change which signaler is responsible for which side (by game, drive, half, or quarter) adds further diversity.

One-Word Play Calls

Regardless of the structure involved in play calling verbiage, there are times when the offense must run plays in as fast as possible. Additionally, many teams that are credited as "Up Tempo" teams (using one-word play calls) in fact only have pieces of their overall plan that is called with singular terms. This offense is no different in that regard, as there is ever-present ability to snap the ball within seconds of the ball being marked "ready for play."

In this system, one-word play calls are referred to as the "Lightning" package. These play concepts are normally foundational ideas in the offense, meaning that the finer coaching points are covered during the normal course of a practice week. Further, it should be noted that these components, because of their prominence as bedrock principles in the overall attack, are suitable in numerous strategic situations.

Why would it be desirable to not have an entire offense on one-word calls? Because the naming convention described in this text allows for more flexibility, not just on a weekly or yearly basis, but on a play to play basis as well. The ability to answer any problem defenses that could be encountered still necessitates multiplicity. In building the Lightning arsenal, it was determined that the following distribution would be utilized:

- 2 Base Runs/ RPOs
- 3 Multi-Purpose Pocket Passes
- 2 Quicks
- 1 Sprint
- 1 Screen
- 3 Deceptive/ Special Plays
- 1 Short Yardage Play

All of the above ideas, as mentioned previously, stem from basic parts of the playbook. Standard calls are simply given abbreviated names with which players can associate.

Figure 4-15. Code: Cornell – Right formation; all break Left.

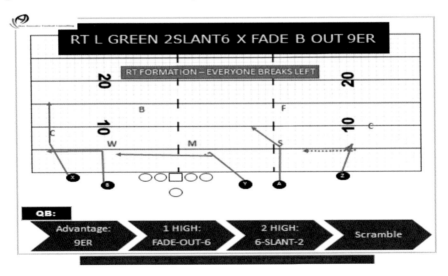

This kind of memory link can be found in most parts of life. For example, when one moves to a new city, turn-by-turn mapping to the mall might be desirable. But as one becomes more accustomed to surroundings, it is likely to clump learning n the following manner: "Where is the restaurant? It's near the mall?" One still wants the flexibility map other locations, but it then becomes possible to commit the familiar to memory.   Figures 4-15 and 4-16 represent examples of quick game packages that can not only be used versus multiple coverage categories, but carry descriptive codes as well.

Figure 4-16. Code: Baylor – Left formation; all break right.

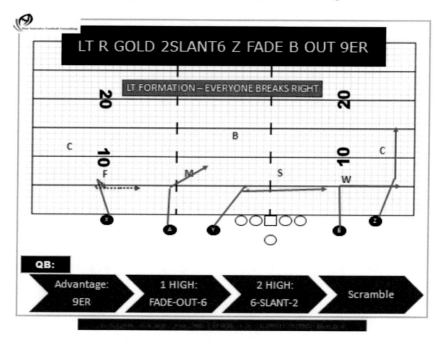

In the above examples, the theme of college names could be used; the position of the "L" and "R" in each name allows for further learning cues – the first direction dictating the formation while the second denotes a feature of the pattern. Setting these elements aside, it is critical to have a defined set of directions for the passer to follow, which will be defined fully in the coming chapters, as the text to this point is so serve as a means to lay the groundwork and provide answers to any defense that might be encountered.

5

Giving the QB Options

Giving the QB Options

At the heart of the matter is the fact that however plays are called, the method for directing the QB's eyes in the passing game is of critical importance. Even at the highest levels of college football, a major criticism of many RPO-based passing games is that quite often, the entirety of the pass offense can surmised in two categories: the RPO and the "bomb" – with no possession passing game to manage the all-important situations where the ball must be passed, either to extend drives or to create high-percentage explosives.

In addition to the above thoughts, the ability to protect (Figure 5-1) consistently with the RPO leaves something to be desired – Jon Gruden once referred to this as the "Ridiculous Protection Offense." Below, there is a reliance on the defense maintaining a 2-high shell; there is also a vulnerability to pressure looks that the defense can utilize. If not judicious in usage, the defense can get a defensive lineman to count as a free rusher, with the quarterback ironically limited in his choices. This counters the intent and potential of the RPO.

Figure 5-1. Popular RPO Example.

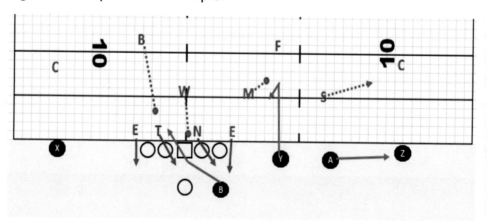

While RPOs are an excellent resource in the offensive arsenal, it is maintained here that they are to be used as a supplemental portion of the passing game, rather than the backbone. Used as a complimentary piece, RPOs can be an invaluable weapon to balance the defense, yet maintain consistency in the offense.

A Complete Reading "Tool Box"

An astute passing game coach wants to arm his passer with the means of attacking any coverage he can encounter, and doing so without bogging him down in the minutia of possibilities. The sophistication of defenses, as they match to the distribution of offensive players in both pre- and post-snap situations, can lead to a paralyzing amount of information. It is for this reason that this passing game has been organized in the fashion it is – to maximize the span of attack for coaches while maintaining a structure that allows players to attack relentlessly, and without hesitation.

Pure Progressions: A.C.T.S. The backbone of a pocket passing game, in this author's estimation, should be one that simultaneously pushes the ball downfield, discourages man coverage, isolates the best ratios, and puts defenders across the field in conflict. The key here is that the timing is set by the first route available, and that passer uses a simple set of determinants to decide to throw or not throw and move on. This is what is meant by the term "pure progression" – the quarterback has a set sequence regardless of the defenses structure.

Pure progressions in this system are taught with the acronym ACTS, which stands for:

"Advantage – Concept – Third Fix – Scramble"

The "Advantage" route represents the route that is thrown in rhythm, and sets the timing of the progression. This feature provides an added dimension over typical pass concepts where the QB is locked solely into a concept (for example, a curl/flat stretch); this design, while simplistic, can actually hinder the decision making of the QB and be the root cause of negative plays (Figure 5-2). Below, the quarterback has a singular read, which is the flat defender on the right (R). A well-prepared defense, despite playing a coverage vulnerable to this combination, can coach the flat defender to slow play the quarterback, opening on an angle to the curl, while poised to break on the out route.

Figure 5-2. Curl/Flat with no Advantage Route.

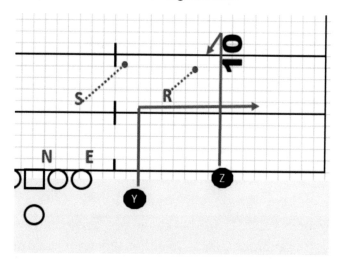

This tactic, in effect, freezes the quarterback, and does things: 1) it causes the ball to be held longer than it should, and 2) it allow S a chance to fly to the curl, eliminating any stretch (Figure 5-3). At the very best, the ball is thrown to the out as the R breaks when the quarterback's top hand comes off the ball, increasing the likelihood of a big hit and a minimal gain. This discouraging result can be seen regularly as defenses pounce on simplistic passing attacks.

Figure 5-3. QB holds the ball; R drives to short route.

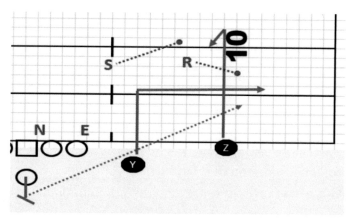

With the defense forced to confront a more explosive possibility before the concept, the passer has not only more varied downfield possibilities, but more room for completions as well (Figure 5-4).

Figure 5-4. Curl/Flat with ACTS thinking.

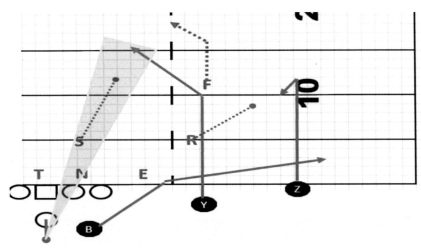

With the QB poised to throw the quick post, both the front side safety (S) and the strong linebacker (S) must honor the threat. The result is an isolated R; though he tries a similar technique as previously described, the stretch is greater because the flat defender is forced to cover more ground.

Figure 5-5. Stretch on flat defender.

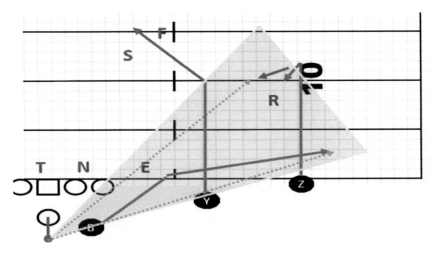

Further, because of the technique of the running back, he is further outside than the slot, creating a true inside-out stretch (Figure 5-5).

Along with the quick post (8 route), there are three other routes that are defined as advantage routes: the 0 (Figure 5-6), the 4 by an inside receiver (Figure 5-7), and the 7 (Figure 5-8).

Figure 5-6. Example of the 0 vs 2 Deep.

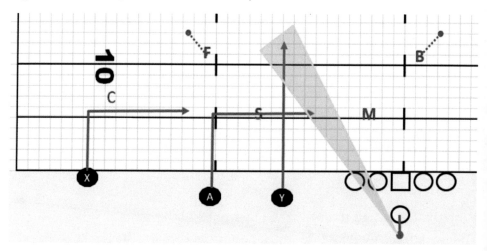

Figure 5-7. Inside "4" versus fast-dropping inside linebackers.

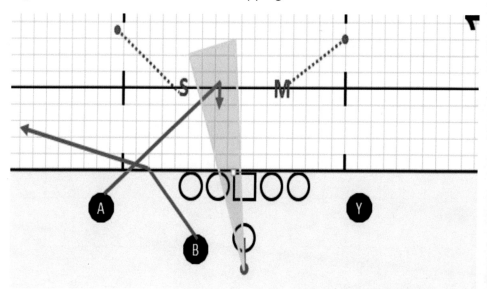

Figure 5-8. "7" route versus man coverage.

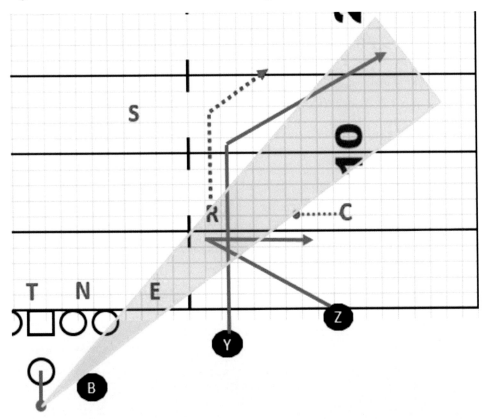

The common theme with all advantage routes is that the decision keys are made available at the snap of the ball for the quarterback, discouraging disguises and late movement, subscribing to the belief that the better the disguise, the more out of position the defenders are at the snap. In the diagram above, for example, the outside receiver's stem is inside, rather than vertical – making the corner declare his intentions. In the traditional "smash" pattern where he runs a hitch, the corner can back up even in man coverage, delaying the decision on the 7/ flag route. More importantly, it allows the offense to dictate, in quick rhythm, isolations in the defense. If the coverage is perfect on the advantage route, the table is then set for the Concept portion of the pattern.

The concepts, in this offense, have three classifications: Stretches, Scans, and Object Reads.

Stretches. A stretch is defined as a 2 on 1 isolation in favor of the offense. The theory here is that with the proper spacing, any 2 offensive players will always defeat a single defender. A stretch is a stretch, whether it is horizontal (Figure 5-9) or vertical (Figure 5-10).

Figure 5-9. "Gold 851 Patriot" - Horizontal stretch on W vs. Cover 4.

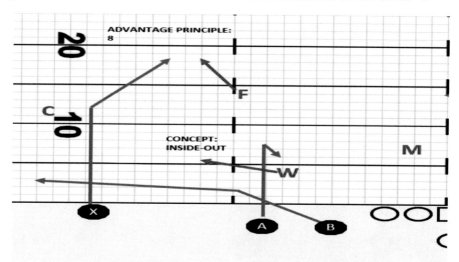

Figure 5-10. "Green 839 Halo" - Vertical Stretch on C vs. Cloud adjustment

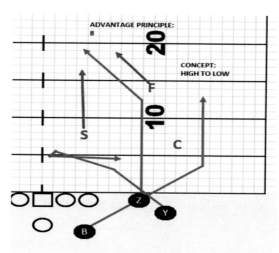

The term for a High-Low thought process for the passer is "HALO". Read tags for horizontal stretches are PATRIOT or DOLPHIN; Patriot reflects the coach's desire for the quarterback to work inside-out (as "I" comes before "O" in the word), while Dolphin conveys the direction to think outside-in ("O" comes before "I" in "Dolphin"). Figure 5-11 demonstrates how a coach, anticipating the 1 route coming free with motion, would want the QB poised for this situation.

Figure 5-11. "Ace Bunch A Mo Brown 731 B-6 Dolphin"

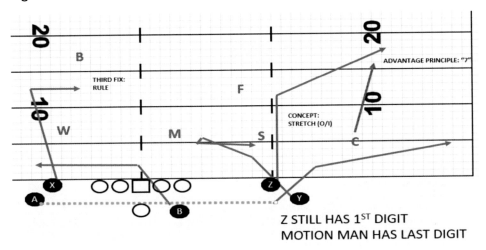

Z STILL HAS 1ST DIGIT
MOTION MAN HAS LAST DIGIT

Scans. A scan read (coded as "Steeler") is utilized with two crossing routes going in the same direction. The quarterback starts his eyes out in front of the first crosser, and moves to the second. As Figure 5-12 illustrates, the play call will often situate the pattern so that as the passer's eyes go from the advantage to the first crosser. Because of this eye movement, the eyes see any interception danger out in front.

The beauty of the scan read is the economy of it, as it is already present in many systems (Figure 5-13). The diagram here shows eye movements that are the same as the Steeler read being discussed. With the ability to take advantage of this already learned skill, there yet another application – the Third Fix, which will be covered later in this chapter.

Figure 5-12. Going from Advantage (Post) to Scan. Post is eliminated, and as eyes move across, QB sees danger players in front of crossing routes.

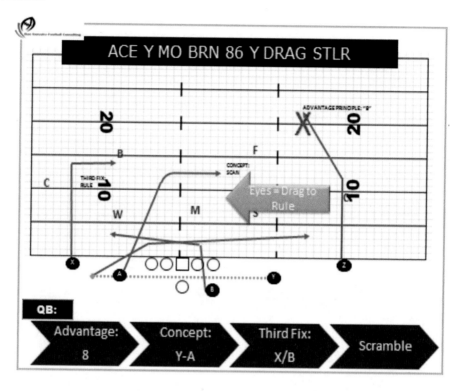

Figure 5-13. Eye Movements from FB to TE= Scan

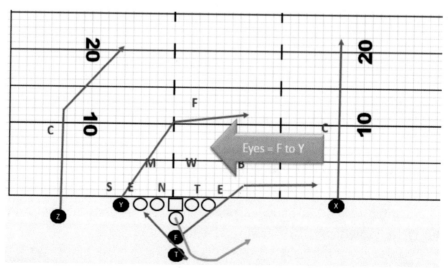

Object Reads. The third type of concept is referred to as an Object Read. While an object receiver is not in a 2 on 1 situation, he is given the opportunity to win because he has 1) route options or 2) a double move (Figure 5-14). The assumption is made that a receiver with multiple route possibilities will defeat a single defender. The term used is GATOR – "Go Advantage, Then Object Read."

Figure 5-14. Types of routes that are Objects.

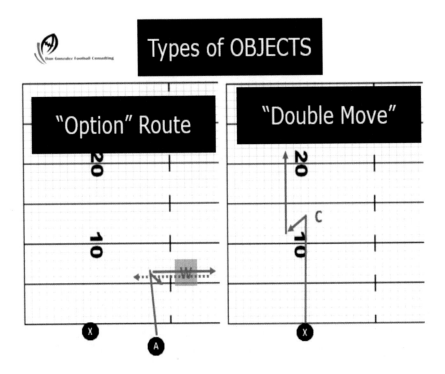

Third Fix. The "Third Fix" in ACTS serves as a means to attack the over-compensation the defense must have created in order to take away both the Advantage and the Concept in a pure progression. In the following scenarios, using a core Lightning (1-word play call), one can see the holes left in order to take away the front (right) side of the field.

Figure 5-15. Sample Pattern: "Lightning 1"

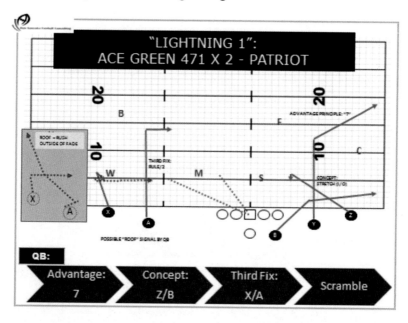

The defense, playing what appears to be Cover 4 pre-snap, sinks the corner, meaning the 7 is eliminated at the snap of the ball. While keeping the corner sinking with his facemask, he knows to hitch or pop up, allowing the 1 route to get to the flat and the 4 to spot up inside of the flat defender (S).

Figure 5-16. Elimination of the Advantage Route.

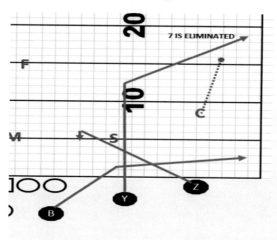

The passer then knows to look for the stretch on the flat defender. However, Mike and Sam match B and Z (Figure 5-17), hence, there is no stretch.

Figure 5-17. Elimination of Concept

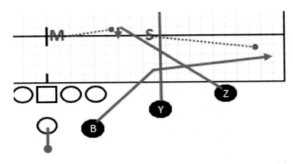

The quarterback is forced to move his eyes to the middle of the field as he hitches up a second time in the pocket. Because of the movement of the Mike, W cannot be right (Figure 5-18). The ball can be thrown to X or A, or pulled down for a scramble. Perhaps as meaningful as anything in the system is the fact that the sequencing of the eyes assures that the passer sees what is out in front of these inside-breaking routes. Because of this feature, the ability to negate disguises pays huge dividends; the total coverage picture is revealed in Figure 5-19; the coverage was not at all what the pre-snap look indicated, but the structure still guides the offense to a completion.

Figure 5-18. Third Fix

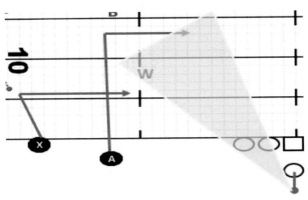

Figure 5-19. Coverage is revealed as strong roll.

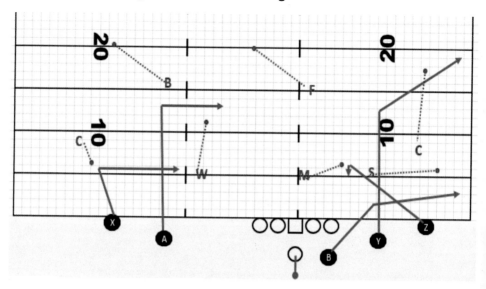

Advantage Principles. If one is to truly maximize an attack via the forward pass, pure progressions <u>cannot</u> be the sole method for directing the quarterback's eyes. Well-coached defenses can be trained, just as the quarterback is coached, to progress through a pass pattern -- most everyone has seen instances where the passer drops back, then checks down, only for the receiver to be hit immediately (and often resoundingly). This is where Advantage Principles play a key role in keeping the efficiency of the offense. Advantage Principles can be thought of a as a "speed reading" version of the progression; the coaching staff will assemble a multi-purpose pass pattern, then designate a means to divide the defense for the QB. Different rhythms can then be used, and the offense can be further diversified. Also, practice time is maximized, as specific patterns only need to be practiced versus specific looks.

Ram. An acronym for "Read Away from Mike," this term divides the underneath coverage and attacks away from the middle linebacker's drop (Figure 5-20). The result could be a stretch or an object read on the next linebacker (Figure 5-21).

Figure 5-20. Matchups away from Mike's Rotation

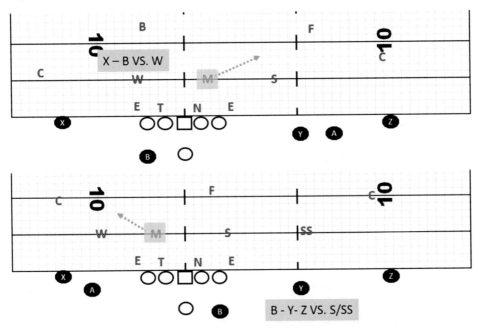

Figure 5-21. Types of isolations: Object (left) and Stretch (Right)

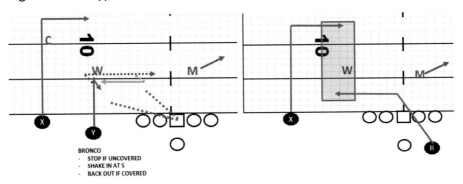

The common theme when using the RAM principle is the isolation; in order to get the proper defender separated, it becomes of critical importance to declare the correct man as the "Mike." This becomes particularly important with the prominence of 3-down fronts that are being used. An excellent starting point would be to begin on the side with 2 releasers. Labeling from the outside-in, the first backer is "Will" and the second is "Mike" (Figure 5-22). There are, of course adjustments,

71

among the most prominent of which will be discussed in the chapter on game planning.

Figure 5-22. Identifying Mike in vs a 3-4 defense.

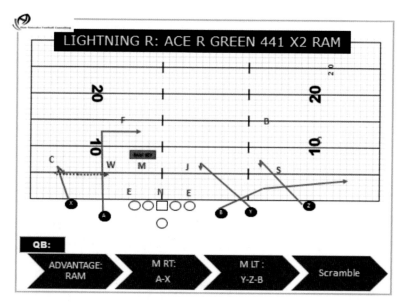

Niner. If RAM divides the defense based on the underneath coverage, NINER separates based on the defensive backfield – more specifically, in terms of 1- or 2- high safety structures. In older pro terminology, this was referred to a "numbers" read (Figure 5-23), which is why the read type was signified with "Niner."

Figure 5-23. Route Conversion vs Cover 3 (left) and Cover 2 (right).

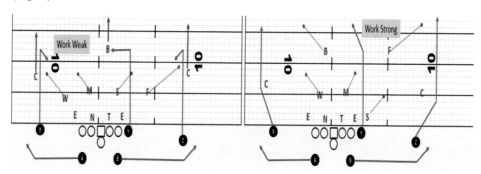

The earliest versions of the concept, rooted in a pro-style approach to route conversion, basically tried to get 5 short receivers vs Cover 3 and three deep receivers vs Cover 2. Obviously, there has been much evolution, even at the high school game, that has made it more difficult to think this way. Pattern reading defenses and split-field coverage techniques can not only confuse the quarterback, but the receivers charged with changing their route as well. As a solution, the approach used here is predicated on the alignment of the boundary safety (Figure 5-24). Further, the terms used in coaching receivers relieve them of identifying the entire field. Instead, they are only asked to beat the leverage of adjacent defenders. This subtlety cannot be overlooked; though the effect on the defense is the same, it reduces mental burden by creating clearer definition, once again allowing players to "play fast."

Figure 5-24. Boundary Safety location to drive decision.

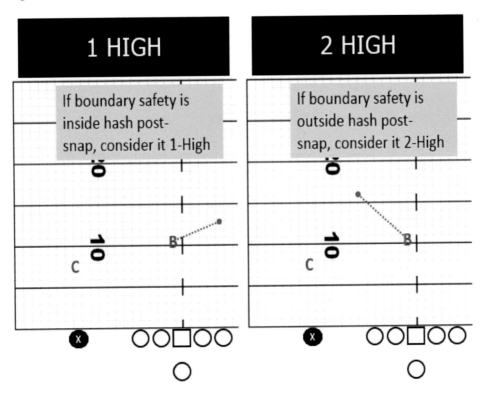

The theory for the Niner Advantage Principle is straight forward. If the safety is inside the hash, it is unlikely that Cover 2 will be encountered to the short side; if he is outside the hash, the corner has deep support, so is capable of rolling up. When there is a weak Cover 2, with B coming off the hash, more room is created in the middle of the field. With the constraint that the ball should be spotted on or near the (college or high school) hash mark, effective patterns can be created that give options versus an array of coverage categories (Figures 5-25). In addition, recognition for all involved than a rigid set of orders that can be easily misread in the heat of battle.

Figure 5-25. Dropback NINER pass.

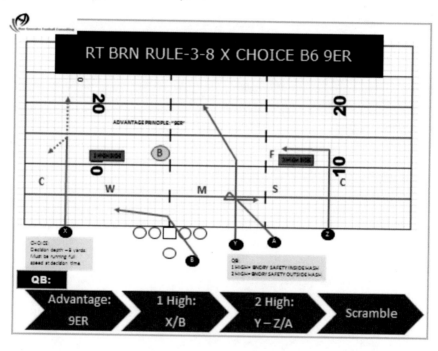

Above, if the safety rotates inside the hash (which can happen even vs. Cover 4 due to Y's vertical release), the following can happen into the boundary (Figure 5-26):

Figure 5-26. Choice possibilities.

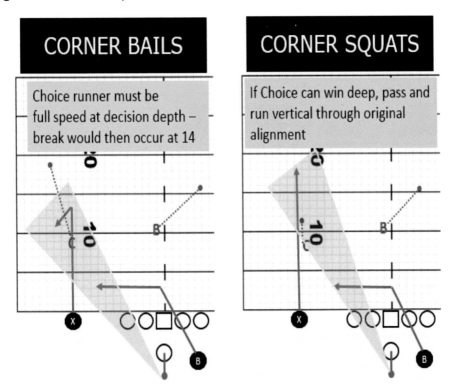

The quarterback, keeping his facemask up the hash, can peek out of the corner of his eye and see the relationship of the corner with and X. He will give an extended 3 step drop with a hitch to be defined. All the while, the B is the outlet should there be no delineation. If, for some reason, the B is chased by M, there is a possibility of moving into the pocket and scanning back to the Y.

If the boundary safety stays outside the hash, the coverage would be considered 2-deep, and the decision is then made to work the frontside of the pattern (Figure 5-27). As soon as B drives off the hash, the ball can be exchanged to the 8 route by Y, based on the drop of the middle linebacker (M). If the M does get underneath Y, the eyes move to the stretch created on the Sam (S) linebacker. It should be noted that the Z must cut underneath the frontside safety, who likely has deep responsibility.

Figure 5-27. Frontside progression.

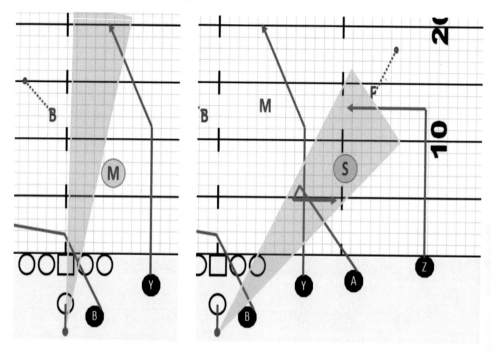

Niner passes are not relegated to 3x1 sets, nor are the reads limited to drop back passes. Figure 5-28 reveals an example of a quick pass. With both sides having passes designed for different types of zone, the play is also tagged with an "Alert," which in this case represents a contingency versus man coverage. Further, there is are both inside and outside fades dialed up to give options versus different man-to-man techniques. On the 1-high side, there is a simple stretch on the W; on the 2-high side, a quick high-low isolation on the M is present, with the X trailing behind. The ALERT is not limited to the diagram, obviously; other selections could be a FADE/OUT combination, or SLANT/FLAT, depending on the skill sets of the players involved.

Figure 5-28. Quick example with "Alert" adjustment.

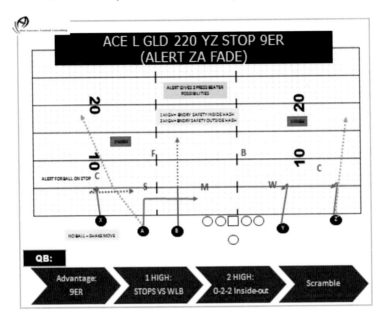

Maverick. This terms stands for "Movement Adjust Vertical or Regular Concept." The idea here is to give an easy key for the quarterback to read for a potential big play, then to go to a normally practiced structure should the defense play it well. There are two primary ways that Maverick tags are presented to the defense; while less conventional than the previous two advantage principles, they owe much of their conception to offenses of the past.

The first method was derived from Dennis Erickson's offenses at Washington State and Miami (Figure 5-29). Using motion to create movement on the part of the defense, the table is set for the passer an instant before the ball is snapped. The goal is to force communication errors on the defensive side; in today's no-huddle world, many defenses are built on automatic calls and are less accustomed to late motion adjustments. If the defense below is geared to have the B key Y and lock the corner on X, how quickly can communication happen with motion outside of X? There is the obvious option to take the vertical to B, but there is also the possibility of the corner bumping with motion, and the safety still reacting strong (5-30).

Figure 5-29. "Maverick" example.

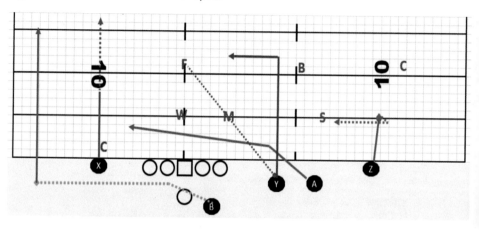

Figure 5-30. Possible weak-side reactions.

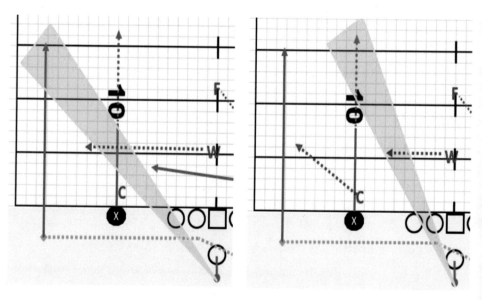

In the event of a perfectly coordinated reaction, the defense is still vulnerable to the common scan read from A to Y to Z (Figure 5-31).

This is an excellent example of adding wrinkles to familiar ideas for the offense.

Figure 5-31. Regular concept.

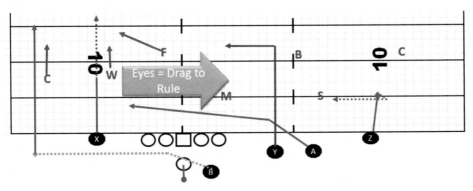

The second presentation of the Maverick tag does not require motion; rather, it relies on quick lateral movement of an outside receiver at the snap (Figure 5-32). This instantaneous, inside movement gives the passer an immediate key against split-field or overload coverage techniques.

Figure 5-32. Maverick without backfield motion.

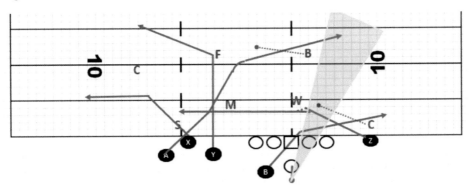

In the diagram above, the initial release of Z makes the corner declare whether he is in man or zone. If the corner chases, that gives the passer the movement adjustment he wants for the vertical play with the back serving as the outlet. If the corner bails, he simply goes frontside, where the distribution of receivers is the same as many basic bunch combinations.

With or without the use of motion, Maverick passes give common pattern structures an added dimension by discouraging overloads and forcing the defense to communicate on the move. This model is particularly useful in today's defensive era where many defenses make automatic checks in order to remain sound against up-tempo offenses. Such adjustments are not only predictable, they allow the offense the chance to dictate terms and create explosive opportunities versus poorly prepared units. Best of all, while the defense must spend an inordinate amount of practice, the pictures for the QB are nothing new!

Cowboy. The fourth of the Four Advantage Principles, Cowboy stands for "Combo or One on One." The major train of thought involving the use of Cowboy involves an isolation route that would be good in attacking single coverage; there is also a pattern component that will take advantage of the defense should they take away the isolation. In other words, in order to double the receiver that the offense is attempting to single up, there will be intentional vulnerabilities elsewhere. And though the idea may seem advanced, the teaching methods are rather elementary.

Figure 5-33. Basic "Cowboy" example.

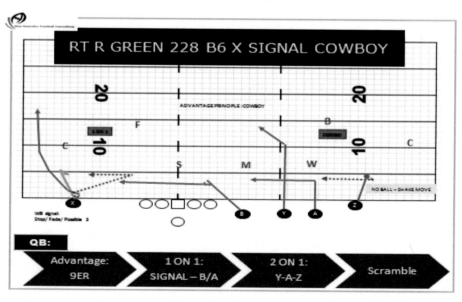

The introductory version of the principle is seen above. The goal of the formation is to make the defense declare its intention; it is obvious that the isolation objective is the single receiver. To the left, the "Signal" route is just that – the desired quick route is signaled at the line of scrimmage in order to remove the possibility for miscommunication. The "combo" route on the strong side of the formation creates a formidable challenge in the event that the defense uses two defenders on X.

Figure 5-34. Two Pass defenders on X.

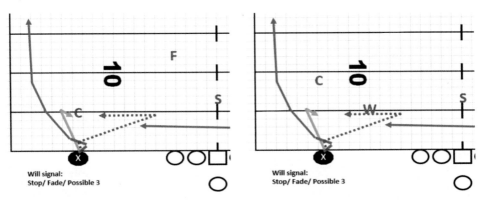

The "Cowboy" read is straight forward; if the defense is deployed with one defender responsible for X, this is where the passer's eyes will start. Should the pre-snap alignment be a mirage, the quarterback still has two crossing routes to scan into – once again, using familiar muscle memory found in other areas of the offense. If the defense puts a 2 pass defenders weak (Figure 5-34), the combo side will be the target.

Figure 5-35. Strong side progression

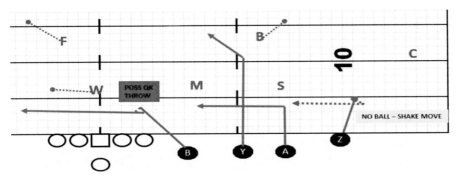

Figure 5-35 gives a magnified look at the strong side of the formation –

the "combo" side. The B provides a potential quick throw, then clears the way so that Y and A can stretch the M. Z's "2" route provides a potential quick throw on his "stop" route, then serves as a late outlet as the route stem breaks inside to the open void behind A. As one will see in the installation section, this is a common theme – the message of familiar pictures for the offensive players.

The Cowboy tag can also present a second train of thought. Very early in the introduction of the offense, routes are introduced in context of the preferred defense. For example, a Seam Read is a zone route, while a "TOP" (a 10-yard Option) is a man route. Using COWBOY, patterns can be assembled in with reference to man/zone thinking. In contrast to NINER, it is not dependent on the safety structure, but rather concentrates on the coverage technique, introducing some very exciting possibilities for the offense. In Diagram 5-36, if man coverage is confirmed on left side, the matchup with the A on the outside linebacker is the target; any form of zone brings the eyes to the seam read, using the back's "2" route as the outlet. Clearly, "1 on 1" can be equated to man coverage, and opens an entirely new dimension in attacking a defense.

Figure 5-36. Man/ Zone application of the COWBOY tag.

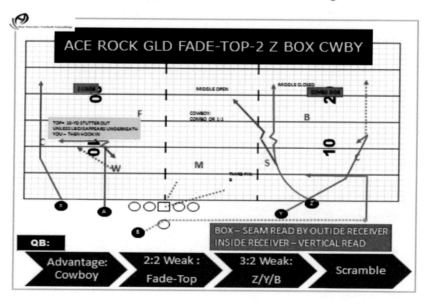

Navigation Tags. Despite a clearly advanced method in communicating and organizing the reads for a quarterback, football is a very fluid game, with countless strategic situations that go beyond standard read rules. It is not hard to imagine the occurrence, at some point, in which extra guidance from the coach is needed in the heat of battle. Further, the in-between-series conversation where the play caller may say "The next time I call this play, try to hit this route" is simply not practicable. For one, it might be the first quarter and the next time that pass is called might be the third quarter. Second, the entire game situation might have changed, requiring a different thought process. Third, the defender that created the opportunity might not even be on the field. For this reason, Navigation Tags were developed. These tags serve the same purpose as a GPS system does for a driver when a normal route is obstructed – a point by point system of directions that guide the passer to the best thought process for that situation. There are five Navigation Tags in this system, each is designed to create a coach-guided override to normal read or progression rules, thus eliminating gray areas for the man with the toughest mental burden on the field.

Figure 5-36. Colt example.

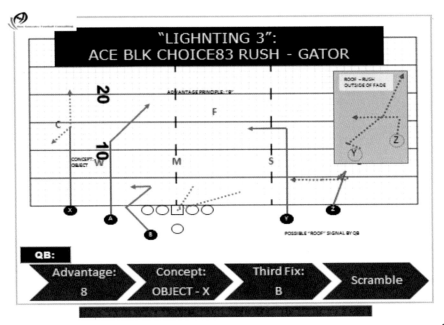

83

Colt. Perhaps the most elementary of the tags, COLT is an acronym for "Call on the LOS." The basic idea is that while the QB is given a thought process with every play call, the play caller reserves the right to override that thought once the defense is aligned. Figure 5-36 shows a basic pattern called in anticipation of blitz or man coverage. The 8 route (post) is available versus a vacant middle, while X's choice route defeats any single coverage technique, and the back's pivot provides an outlet.

If, however, the coverage look is different than anticipated – a boundary zone blitz look (Figure 5-38), for example, the play caller can override the thought process at the line. Knowing the rotation that will both move the protection rules and keep the B in from releasing, the direction to the QB could possibly be to "RAM" read this play; the quarterback is the only one needing this signal, since the rest of the offense is set in their assignment. Once the thought process is communicated, the eyes simply go away from Mike; with the backside safety rotating into the deep middle, there is a clear isolation on S. The result is an accelerated means of getting to the backside of the pattern, and hitting the defense where it is weakest. True to the root meaning of the word "coach" – derived from "stage coach" – the play caller is able to steer the field personnel to the optimum lanes of completion.

Figure 5-38. "COLT" – read changed to RAM.

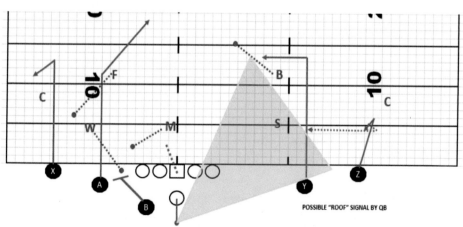

POSSIBLE "ROOF" SIGNAL BY QB

Cobra. Code for "Come off to Best Runner Available," the COBRA navigation tag allows the flexibility of bypassing every sequence of the progression to get the ball to the offense's most gifted run after catch (RAC) athlete. COBRA basically tells the quarterback to think of optimizing the advantage route, and then find a way to drop the ball off for the RAC. It goes without saying that a clear line of communication is needed between the coaching staff and the quarterback, so that the player is identified. For example (assuming the RB is identified as a team's best "RAC" guy), the play below (Figure 5-39) features a basic pattern in the offense, but giving the clear instruction that absent of a wide open "Crooked 0" route by Y (blue vision triangle), the ball will be dropped off to B (green vision triangle).

Figure 5-39. Basic pattern with COBRA navigation tag.

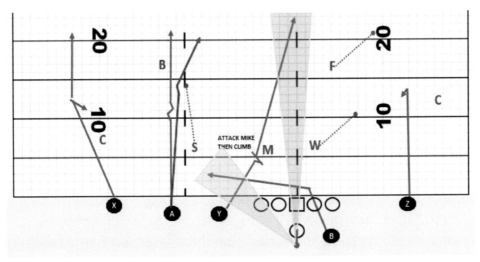

There can, of course, be specialty patterns built specifically for COBRA calls. In the diagram below, one sees how a "perfect" motion adjustment by the defense can actually play into the offense's plans. The previous point had been made about the inside release of a route outside of a "7;" here, the offense invites soft coverage, both with motion and with the stem of the B's route. The QB will coached to throw the 2 to the running back vs. soft coverage – the stem of the Z helps clear the runway inside.

If press or a rolled up corner is present, the 7 protects against that; followed by an inside high-low combination.

Diagram 5-40. Specialty COBRA pattern.

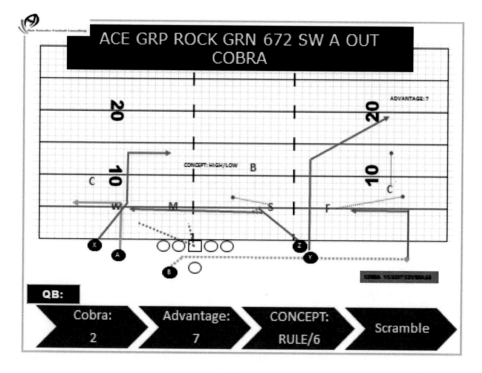

Falcon. The "Falcon" tag brings situational overrides into the passer's thought process. Standing for "Forget the Advantage, Look Off to Concept," the coach, on a play-by-play basis can choose to determine when the deep shots are eliminated from the progression according to the game situation. For example, on a critical 3rd down, the coaching staff might want an immediate, high percentage throw for the first down rather than the pure progression read that could result in a big play (Figure 5-41). The coaching staff should always have the ability to not only make this determination, but communicate this intention as well. The ability to toggle on and off the Advantage Route further removes the unproductive sideline conversations on the topic of "What were you thinking?" – when the player was almost assuredly trying to hit a big play.

Figure 5-41. FALCON override on normal progression.

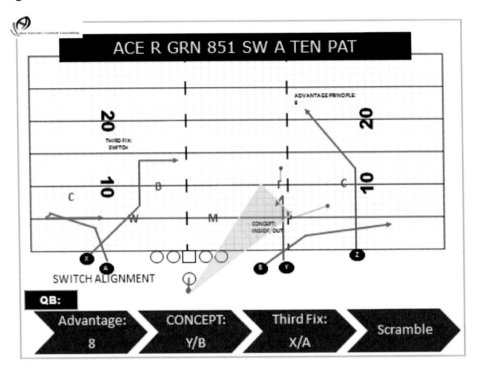

Above, this pass (the offense's version of "Stick") was part of the 2018 Day 1 Installation Plan. As one can readily see, the chance to hit the 8 route by Z might be tempting because of the slow retreat of the frontside safety (F). However, because of the heavy inside leverage of the corner, it could take more time to cross that player's face. Knowing this, the offensive play caller, on a 3rd & 6 might want to use the FALCON navigation tag, which removes the 8 from consideration. The QB will look off to the 8, knowing he will use work the inside-out stretch on the flat defender. The benefit here is the added time it might have taken for Z to win would allow M to become a factor on the play the offense really needs – which it the throw for the first down conversion. The player is absolved of having to hold the ball, and can simply play for to keep the drive alive by working the Y/B stretch, or the backside combination if M simply flies to get underneath the route by Y.

Raider. An acronym that communicates to "Read the Advantage then to backside In/Under," this tag has extreme value in getting the quarterback's eyes all the way across the field, without losing the possibility of the explosive play. While RAM divides the defense based on the M linebacker's drop, the eyes inside could develop dangerous habits, as it would slow the reading of an Advantage Route.

Diagram 5-42. RAIDER tag to get the passer's eyes backside.

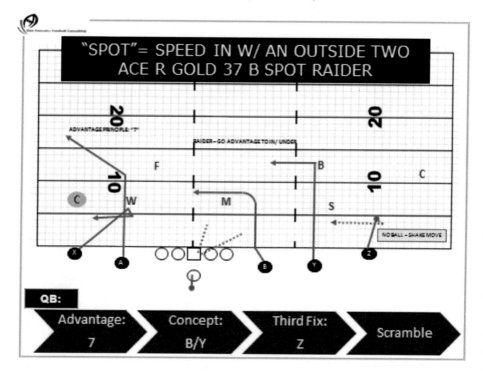

Diagram 5-42 reveals an example of how the RAIDER tag moves the passer's eyes. Rather than a pure high low on the corner to the offense's left, there is just the decision to throw the 7 to A or move on. Basically, any retreating corner would direct the eyes to a backside high-low. All the while, the eyes will see the interception danger in front of crossers. The ability to eliminate or throw to an individual route, then be made aware of going to a backside combination threatens the entirety of the defense in short order.

Texan. While much of these navigation tags allow the quarterback the means to find the most high percentage throw, Texan removes the guesswork from the potential situation of the QB coming off of the potential deep shot too early. "Texan" communicates the play caller's desire to think in terms of "touchdown to check down;" in the context of time, there is the ability to use all the time that would have gone to the Advantage and then the Concept, before finally settling on the Third Fix in the progression. Basically, the focus becomes getting the explosive shot (Figure 5-43).

Figure 5-43. TEXAN tag to communicate the shot portion of a play.

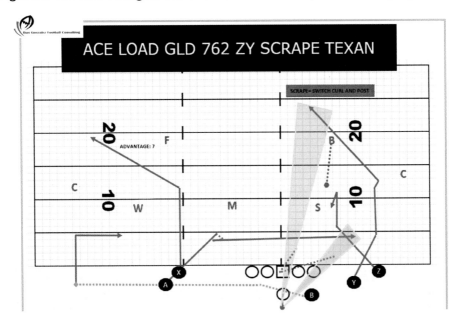

The diagram above shows a possible throw to the switch-post vs. Cover4; the Texan navigation tag gives the order to give extra attention to the possibility of the deep throw, but to come down to the Third Fix should that fail to materialize. The logic must always remain that the time available is finite, and that if extra allowance is given to one part of the progression, an element must be subtracted elsewhere. Even when departing from the normal thought process, gray areas are eliminated.

The elimination of "gray areas" means the elimination of doubt, and Navigation Tags remove any doubt of the intentions of the play caller. The elimination of doubt increases decisiveness, which is the hallmark of great leadership – a must from the quarterback position. Further, Navigation Tags (along with the primary read methods available) bring a level of accountability that is not always present; a coach cannot simply dial up a pass play and hope for the best, then question what the quarterback saw if results are lacking.

6

A Plan for Installation

A Plan for Installation

To this point, it has been demonstrated how a passing system can be constructed to not only maximize the ability of the receiving group, but the capacity of the quarterback as well. However, no structure can bring about the desired results without the proper installation and practice planning. Many systems, as well as promising talent, have been spoiled by the failure to appropriately layer teaching; more still have been spoiled by inadequate practice planning or situational preparation. With the groundwork now laid in previous chapters to have an understanding of the flexibility that can be achieved, it is perhaps more important to understand how to issue in learnable chunks.

The Installation Schedule. The key to execution, in the opinion of this author, lies in the number of quality repetitions that can be refined over time. This belief is what drives the philosophy that there is no new learning during the season, and that all concepts and adjustments are presented over the spring and summer in order to be able to maximize their effectiveness during the most critical times. Combining the ease in initial learning of the passing system with the situational components that are built into the system, the installation track can be visualized accordingly:

Figure 6-1. Theoretical Model

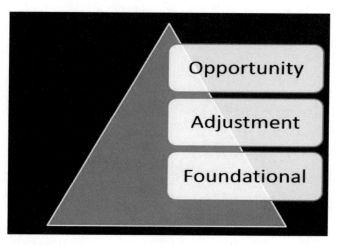

Both run and pass games are looked at in this manner, and in doing so, a methodical, structured approach to teaching can be established. With this mindset, it can also be determined whether or not a new idea is profitable, and whether or not it will get the practice repetitions necessary to be set for success. The totality of this passing system can be taught in six installation segments, which obviously plays on the fact that the teaching is layered. In other words, each technique builds off of another, and is applicable in many different facets of the overall scheme. The benefits of such an approach are abundant. From the standpoint of the passing game, the ability to create the same pictures for the passer cannot be overstated. For example, the ability to start eyes out in front of a crossing route, and then move them into the break, is a common theme in this offense. Let the following examples prove the point:

Figure 6-2. Eyes into a backside Third Fix

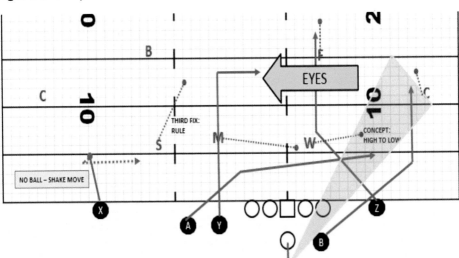

As the eyes move from the concept (B on a 9 and A on a drag), they not only anticipate Y, but see where M is as well; with the "banjo" the M and S linebackers execute, M chases the first crosser, leaving S behind the Rule route by Y.

Figure 6-3. Eyes to in route off of NINER Advantage Principle

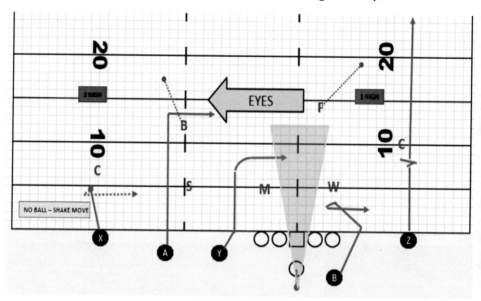

In Figure 6-3, using NINER, the frontside safety (F) expands off the hash, denoting "2 High". The eyes drop down to see the relationship between the speed in and the M, and then scan to the A if the M maintains leverage.

Figure 6-4. Movement protecting from interception danger,

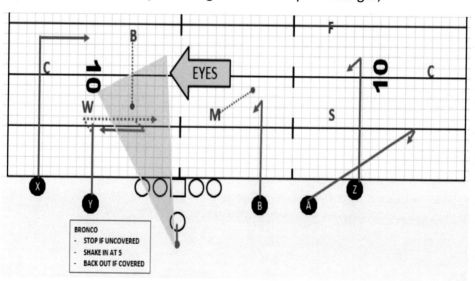

In the standard LIGHTNING call diagrammed above, the QB is taught to use the RAM Advantage Principle. At the snap, M expands, and the passer keeps him going in that direction with his eyes, knowing he is creating space for his intended target, the Bronco (option) route by the Y. As his eyes move, he sees the trap being set by the defense, as the backside safety is dropping down to rob the option. Because the movement of the passer's eyes allow for this vision, he is able to reset and throw to X. The number of times over the years that this has occurred cannot be understated – even with a junior high QB. Further, this situation could happen all the way inside the 5-yard line, where the Rule route by X would work the back line.

Despite being in different stages in the progression sequence, or possibly different depths or with different receivers, the kinesthetic memory and the "picture" in the quarterback's brain are firmly entrenched; these pictures, once in place, can last a lifetime. It is not uncommon for a grown adult to remember visions from childhood, whether it was a first Little League home run or the position of the ball in the air when one realizes "oh no!" on an interception. The volume of offense demonstrated here is made possible because of these pictures, and the face that strict definitions are created by Advantage Routes/ Principles. The results are the execution of high-definition decision-making and increased accuracy due to the ability to anticipate the next man in the progression. The key to teaching then, becomes the sequence in which ideas are installed; moreover, the packaging of concepts must allow for carry over across a wide array of strategic situations. Within the aforementioned six segments for installation, it should be noted that the first three lay the complete foundation, while the remaining three focus on situational calls. In addition, the elements introduced in Install 1 have their adjustments in Install 4; variations to Install 2 come in Install 5, and so forth. As a result, not only are situational elements covered, but also the basic principles are, in effect, installed twice.

Figure 6 – 5. Installation theory

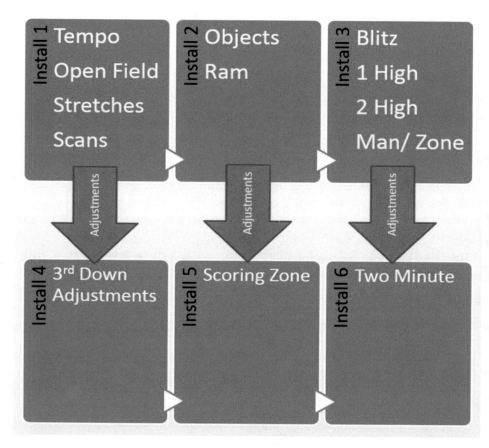

Install #1. First, from a protection standpoint, the half man/ half slide scheme is installed, with all three versions (Figure 6-6). Because there is no new learning for the offensive line, it is important to prepare the offense for the array of combinations that will occur during the course of a season. With this same train of thought, calls that condense splits and create many of the movement possibilities previously discussed are introduced here (Bunch/ Stack alignments and motion) – the reason being that if that is how the offense will play in "must win" situations, that is how the offense will be taught from the onset. In terms of reading principles, the ACTS (pure progression) theory is introduced; the three stretch tags are all presented here, along with the scan principle, as it is integral to multiple facets of the offense.

Figure 6-6. Protection summary

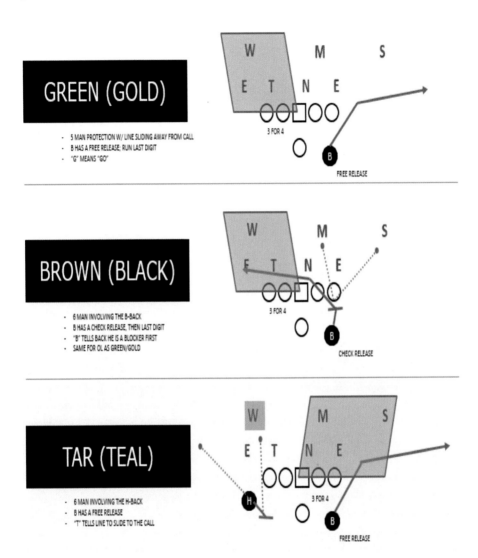

GREEN (GOLD)

- 5 MAN PROTECTION W/ LINE SLIDING AWAY FROM CALL
- B HAS A FREE RELEASE; RUN LAST DIGIT
- "G" MEANS "GO"

3 FOR 4

FREE RELEASE

BROWN (BLACK)

- 6 MAN INVOLVING THE B-BACK
- B HAS A CHECK RELEASE, THEN LAST DIGIT
- "B" TELLS BACK HE IS A BLOCKER FIRST
- SAME FOR OL AS GREEN/GOLD

3 FOR 4

CHECK RELEASE

TAR (TEAL)

- 6 MAN INVOLVING THE H-BACK
- B HAS A FREE RELEASE
- "T" TELLS LINE TO SLIDE TO THE CALL

3 FOR 4

FREE RELEASE

In terms of routes and pattern structures, the 7, 8, and SEAM advantage routes are taught in terms of timing, landmarks, and keys (Figures 6-7 through 6-9), and are put in conjunction with backside tags that represent four of the seven route structures: Drags and Trails (Figure 6-10), 7s – Frontside (Figure 6-11), Turn/Curl Flat (Figure 6-12) and Wheel/Drag (Figure 6-13).

Figure 6-7. "7" (Flag) advantage route w/frontside stretch.

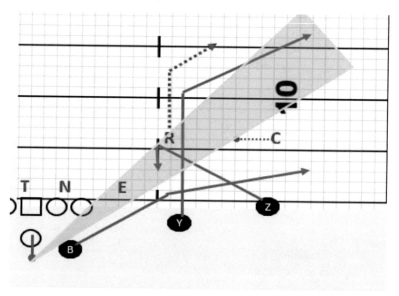

Figure 6-8. "8" (Post) Advantage with Scan

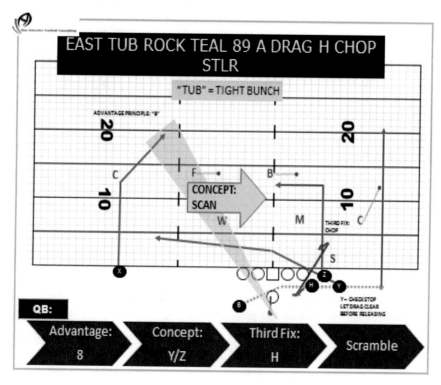

Figure 6-9. "SEAM" Advantage with High-Low Stretch

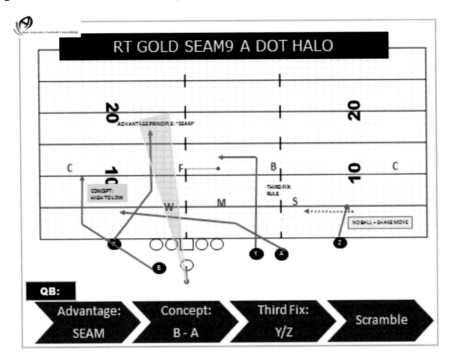

Figure 6-10. Drag/Trail Definition

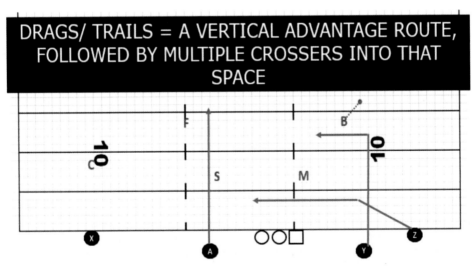

Figure 6-11. "7" with Frontside Concept definition.

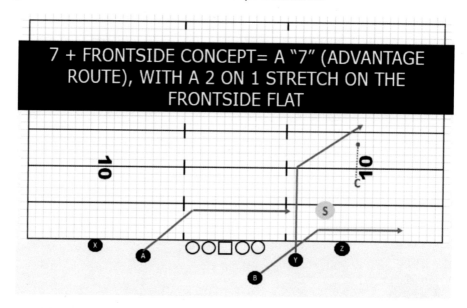

Figure 6 -12. Turn/Curl-Flat Structure

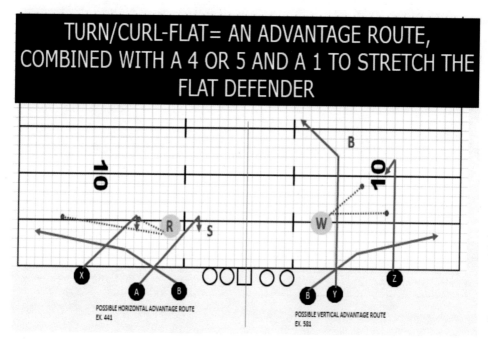

Figure 6-13. Wheel-Drag components

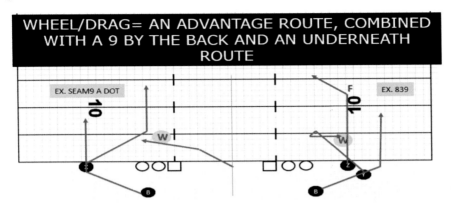

In terms of backside tags, previously discussed RULE and SWITCH tags are of taught, in addition to individual tags for DRAG (6-14) and TEN (6-15) routes for inside receivers, as well as the apparatus for tagging the B-back at the end of a call (6-16). Moreover, verbiage rules are introduced; tags that end in "OT" such as DOT tell the outside receiver on that side to run a "2" – "A DOT" means "A Drag, Outside Man run a 2 (Figure 6-17)."

Figure 6-14. Individual DRAG tag.

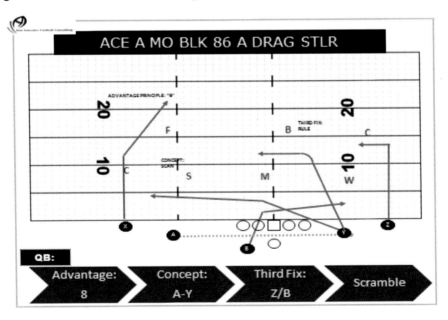

Figure 6-15. Individual TEN example: Switch A Ten

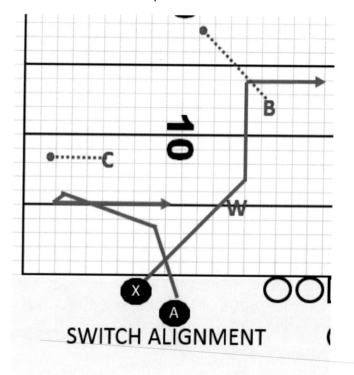

Figure 6-16. "B" TAG (Ex. LEFT BLACK 585 B6 NINER)

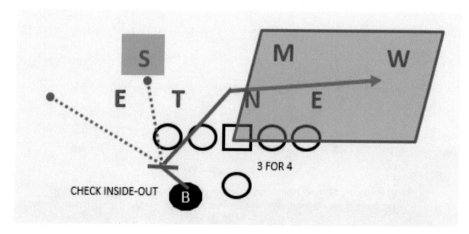

Figure 6-17.   DOT Tag: "Drag with an Outside 2"

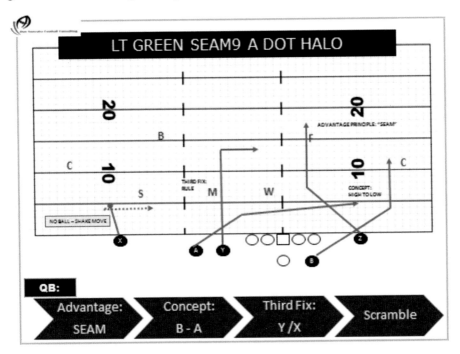

Because of the emphasis on tempo – both in terms of how to conduct practice as well as in terms of execution – two LIGHTNING calls, featuring a run and a pass, will be introduced. The run will simply be the code word(s) for the featured scheme on Day 1, while the pass would be a coded version of a basic pass. There are no extra repetitions involved here, other than the offense being indoctrinated to multiple tempos during group and team practice periods.

Install 2. In the second installation period, the primary supplementary features to the drop back game are installed (Figure 6-18). From a protection standpoint, complimentary actions such as sprint or play action protections are to be installed. With the primary pocket protection schemes already introduced in the first practice, the remaining teaching in this regard becomes different situational adjustments; technique here is of paramount importance.

The route packages involve the addition of the "0" (locked seam) as an advantage route, along with the core of the adjusting routes in the pass offense. The emphasis here obviously builds off of previous teaching, as the subtleties in eye movements keep building off of mental pictures created for the quarterback. For instance, the "0" route, though seemingly the most basic read and throw, comes at a slightly faster rhythm than the SEAM; becoming accustomed to seeing the SEAM with its longer stem allows for better assimilation (Figure 6-19).

Figure 6-18. Install 2 snapshot.

#	Sit	Prot	FS Combo	Tags	Read
2		Sprint: Slate/ Straw	7 Combos (BS): - 671 (or 761) 0 Combos (* RAM):	Bronco Beam/ Box A 3	Object: - Gator
		Zone Slide: Reno/ Lincoln	- 506 - Rush-Swirl-6 B-0 - *200	Swirl	Mike: - Ram
			Ram (FS) - 5Bronco (1x3) - 55FLARE Sprint - 731 (Bun A/Y Mo) - 89Swirl (3x1)		

Figure 6-19. Comparing the "0" and SEAM stems.

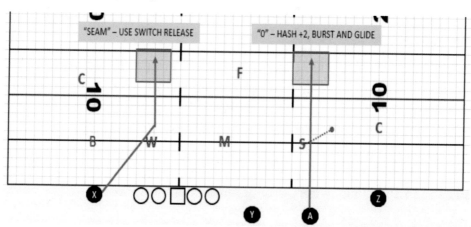

The summary table shows that the applications for the "0" are two-fold. First, there is the obvious application as the frontside companion to the seam read (Figure 6-20), while the route is also used in the possession passing game to give the Drag/ Trail structure an added dimension. Two examples (Figures 6-21 and 22) are given here.

The Seam Read in this offense is an invaluable route versus zone coverage, yet limited against man coverage; because of this, there is the belief that greater variety must be given on the frontside. In addition to the aforementioned locked seam on the frontside, the application of a frontside 7 (Figure 6-23) is vital. Once again, there is an added aspect to previous teaching, as the thought process of going from an advantage route to a backside concept is added, whereas initial teaching involved going from the "7" to a frontside concept. Going frontside to backside has the effect of thinning out the defense, as defenders cannot lean to the passer's initial eye movement.

Figure 6-20. Frontside seam with backside Seam Read.

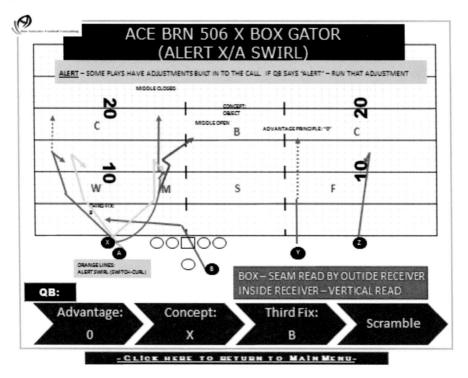

Figure 6-21. Drag/ Trail Example 1

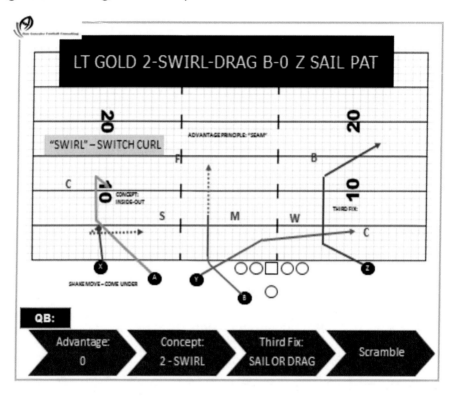

Figure 6-22. Drag/ Trail Example 2

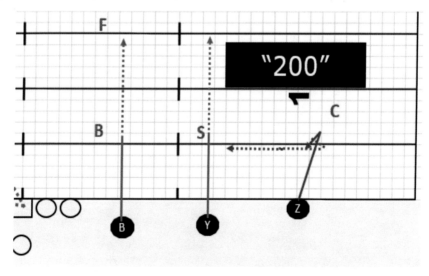

Figure 6-23. "7" (blue triangle) with a backside concept (green triangle).

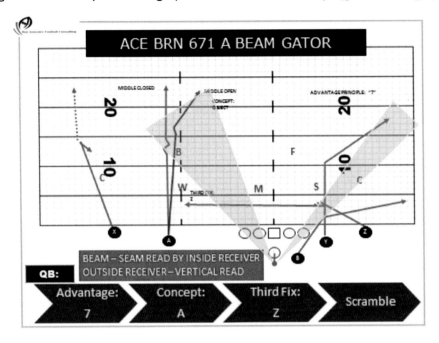

There is, with this teaching, not only the ability to affect more coverage categories, but the ability to isolate defenders more effectively as well. Above, the passer's eyes to the 7 route can hold the F, creating more space for the Seam Read versus the backside safety (B). The crosser from Z not only gives a key for the decision on the Advantage Route (the 7), but serves as a means to control the W as well. In other words, the Seam Read will defeat different forms of zone coverage, and the frontside will defeat man, or serve as a look-off that will draw defenders away from the seam read.

Along with the Seam Read, the "Bronco" route (Figure 6-24), this offense's parlance for an option route, is introduced in the second installation, thus defining the two main conversion routes in the system. While it is important to have the strict adherence to locked Advantage Routes to facilitate timing, it is equally integral to modern pass offense that route stems have the ability to adjust to different techniques.

Figure 6-24. Bronco route.

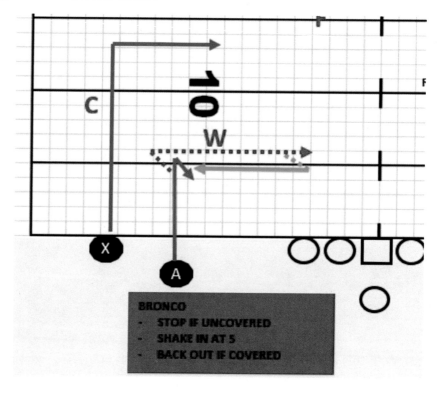

As one can see from the close-up below, the instruction allows for the QB to isolate the option route via the RAM advantage principle (Figure 6-25), then anticipate the quicker of the two breaks, and then adjust to the conversion. If the tagged player is uncovered by alignment, he simply runs a 5 yard stop route. With a player deployed to cover the option, this first move is to win on a shake-in. The shake move is critical for a slot, as it allows the passer to keep the Mike moving away, ensuring isolation. If the option runner is denied leverage by the defender, he whips back out, and the ball is delivered. With this method of teaching, the receiver is unencumbered by having to determine the exact coverage category – once again, allowing for faster play.

Figure 6-25. Example of a full pattern Bronco.

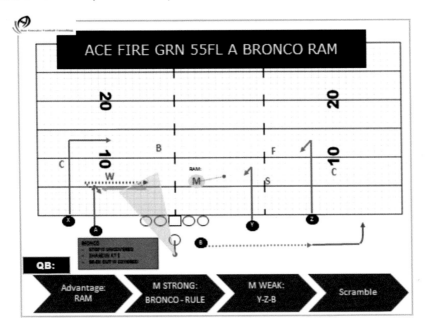

Lastly, Install 2 marks the introduction of the "Alert" concept. "Alert" is a term that denotes an adjustment to the play to make sure the offense "has the chalk last." The adjustment could involve the blocking or protection scheme, a route adjustment, or total play concept, as described by the individual play call. For example, in the play below, there is the normal frontside to backside thinking outlined previously, with the chance to hit a 7 route versus man, and then work the seam read as the object versus Cover 2 or 3. However, there are instances (such as soft, heavy inside leverage on the safety over the seam read) in which a better route combination can be made available. Here, with the "ALERT Y/Z RULE" tag, the possibility of having three viable backside targets is gained, as the outside vertical is a throw that not all quarterbacks can make, making the route nothing more than a clearing route. With the heavy, inside positioning of the backside (B) safety, there is the chance for him to take away both the seam and post adjustments, leaving no real stretch. To alleviate this possibility, the QB would simply call "ALERT! ALERT!" at the line of scrimmage, which in this case takes the

Y and Z and puts them on RULE routes. The QB then can then assure himself of a numbers improvement in his favor – all the while using a basic part of the offense, and a read that is, as demonstrated, central to the attack in general. He can now work from the Y to the Z, with the crosser from X as the outlet if the corner bails, taking away the Advantage 7.

Figure 6-26. Example of "Alert" call in the passing game.

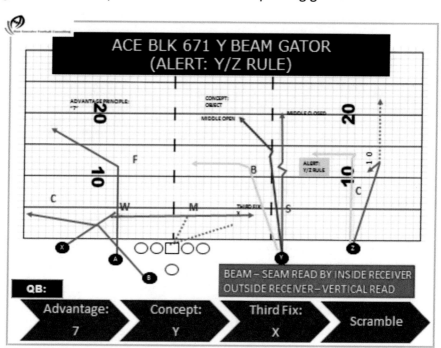

Install 3. With the primary straight progression concepts in place, it is now time to add to the idea of split field Advantage Principles – Niner and Cowboy are introduced, along with the first Navigation Tag – Raider. Though perhaps not used as often as Falcon and Cobra during the season, Raider fits in with the pattern combinations that are being, or have been, introduced. For example, the below Day 1 pass (Figure 6-27) can be augmented to put eyes on the Advantage, then directly to the backside In/Under. It is important to note that the passer's facemask to the Z will

play an integral part in moving M and F, thus creating space for the backside inside-breaking routes, whereas going directly backside might not have the same effect, and will certainly eliminate an explosive play to the quick post.

Figure 6-27. Using "Raider" Navigation Tag to change pattern intent.

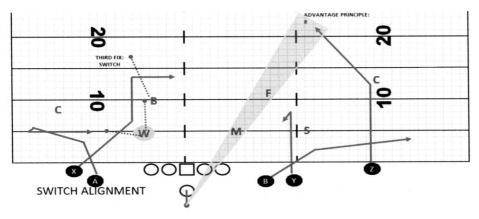

In terms of how the Niner and Cowboy principles are installed, players are given a lesson in key combinations that are desired, both in terms of 1 High/ 2 High and Man/Zone.   Much of the quick game is structured this way, as in Figure 6-28.

Figure 6-28. Quick game Niner pattern.

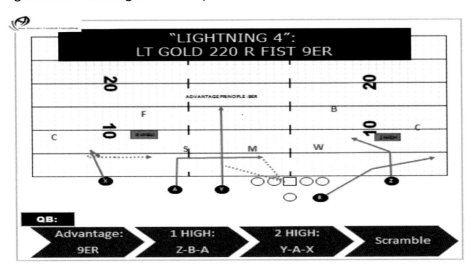

Above, one can see that the "220" combination to the left of the formation is identified as a key 2-Deep "beater" in the quick game. The thinking here is that the #3 receiver is in a position to be inside the field safety (F), thus putting the stretch on the M linebacker, with the outside receiver trailing in behind. Once again, the mental picture for the quarterback is familiar, as the eyes start out in front of the first crosser, then move into the second. And, as the backside safety sets the table for the side of the formation that will be targeted, the offense is assured the backside safety cannot affect a throw to the locked seam. If he does cross the hash, it denotes a single-high look, which is tailor-made for the Slant/Flat combination.

Whatever quick combination is used versus a single-high look, whether it be an individual "Signal" route, or some form of "Stop" route combination (Figure 6-29), some form of inside advantage route with a trail combination provides a solid 2-deep combination, and lends itself to familiarity.

Figure 6-29. Single safety coverage quick combinations.

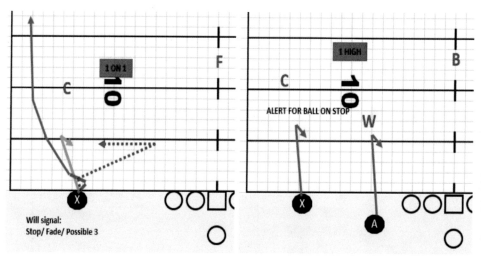

When presenting a 4-receiver surface to the defense, slight variations give the passer the same look, should the B safety expand off the hash (Figure 6-30).

Figure 6-30. 2-Deep combination out of "Quads"

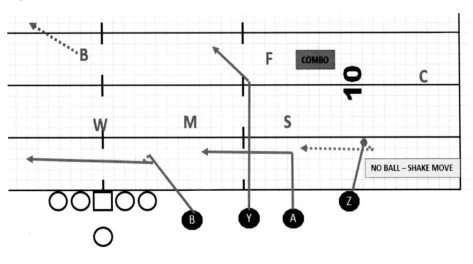

Using the #4 receiver to attract an underneath defender clears the way for the first underneath route; there is the added benefit of serving as an outlet, should the quarterback begin on the single receiver side. The third receiver (Y) should be sent on an 8 route in order to affect the same area as the #3 in trips would, in order to create the same stretch on the M linebacker. There is, of course, the same effect of a trailing under route by the outside receiver.

In the drop back game, it is not hard to imagine potential single-high beaters to use to the single receiver side; just a few possibilities are illustrated in Figure 6-31. With the boundary safety spinning into the middle of the field, there is a great likelihood of a zone featuring a soft corner, or man to man coverage.   Either way, the availability of the single receiver's route can be assessed by the actions of the weak-side linebacker (W).   Of course, the wide variety of combinations is made possible with the use of a numbered tree.

Figure 6-31. Dropback patterns versus 1-High Safety defenses.

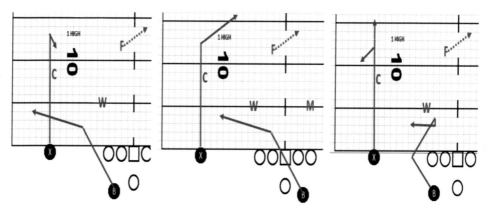

To the "Trips" side, there are 3 main thoughts versus 2 Deep in the drop back game.   Figure 6-32 shows a staple out of a static environment that is called SPOT in this offense, which is an acronym for "Speed In with an Outside Two."

Figure 6-32. SPOT combination.

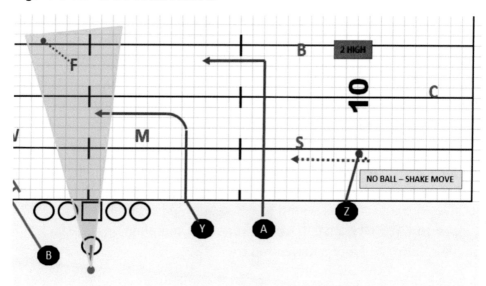

As the passer has his eyes on the safety, seeing him rotate off the hash, they can scan into the Speed In. From there, the well-documented scan read is executed. When using motion, the use of the Bronco route is utilized (Figure 6-33), giving the opportunity to use an option route off of motion and also maintain a vertical release by the eventual #3 receiver, which will help declare defensive intentions. Moreover, there is the added benefit of having the Bronco not being reliant on the RAM principle; this application provides a framework to still use the route versus 3-down defenses where isolating Mike might be more difficult – again, without having to teach something new.

Figure 6-33. Bronco route with motion to Trips.

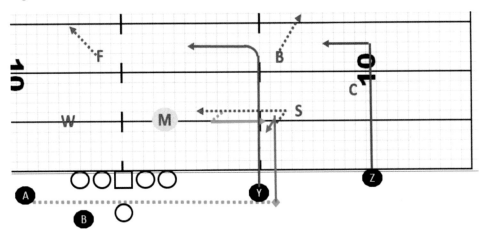

The third thought for some form of 2-deep beater would involve a more vertical possibility against the field safety (Figure 6-34). Though there are many possible alternatives, it would behoove the offense to make this component as cost effective as possible in terms of practice repetitions.

Figure 6-34. Vertical 2- Deep alternative

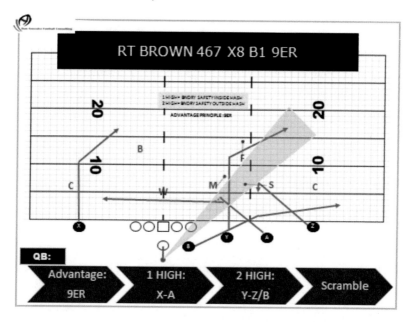

The combination chosen here has several components. First, it overloads the field with four releasers to the strong side. Second, the combination between 2 and 3 looks to the Sam, Mike, and F safety like several other combinations in the offense where #2 gets the ball. Third, "match" coverage can be attacked because of what amounts to a "free run" on the F safety by the Y receiver; Sam and Mike are playing banjo coverage, and with the corner manned up on the Z, there is a great opportunity to hit the 7 route by Y.   Fourth, versus pure zone concepts, this pattern has the exact same distribution as the first idea installed, referred to as "471."

Install 3 is also the introduction point for the second application of the COWBOY thought process, as outlined previously. The TOP route, standing for "10-yard Option," fits into not only the COWBOY Advantage Principle, but the simple application of how worded routes are easily assimilated into our verbiage as well (Figure 6-35).

Figure 6-35. Seam-9-Top

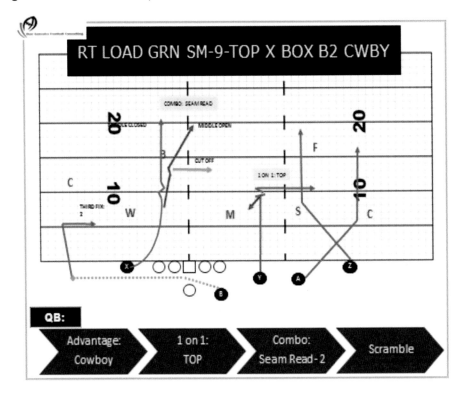

Moreover, the TOP route is an example of how adjustable routes can be taught with simple terms (Figure 6-36). As the diagram below intimates, the receiver simply takes the best release and runs the shake-out unless the defender takes a zone drop underneath him. This would signify zone coverage, and the route runner would then hook to the inside.

At the end of the third installation phase, all of the key components of the offense have been introduced. The final portion that is addressed at this juncture is that of problem defenses; this would include popular pressure schemes and unique looks.

Figure 6-36. Individual TOP route.

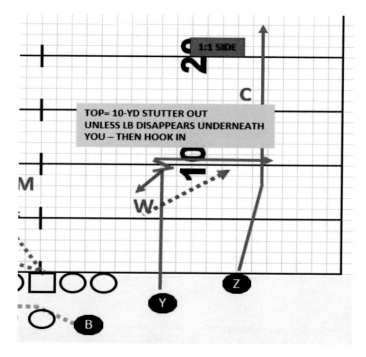

With base runs and protections having been taught, it then becomes critical to apply these rules to defenses such as the "Bear" (Figure 6-37). Normal 3- and 4- down rules require specific adjustments, as the all linemen are covered, eliminating double team possibilities. There is not only the force single blocks in the passing game, but there is obvious benefit at the college and high school levels, as Bear is an effective front versus the zone read. Moreover, the man coverage typically associated with this front is a popular answer versus RPOs. Because of this versatility, devoting early parts of practice to pressure schemes and unique looks also tests the rules being taught and builds confidence in the system.

Figure 6-37. Protection adjustments vs. Bear Front.

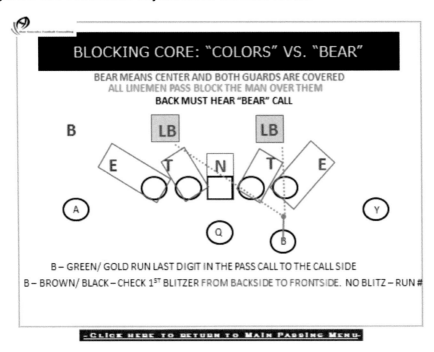

Install 4 through 6. The focus of the following three installation segments is devoted to situational football. As previously explained, adjustments to basic routes structures are introduced as well. With tempo, structure, and the culture of offense being the key facets of the first three installation practices, the last three can emphasize how these ingredients can prove to be the major propellants of success during the critical stages of a football game.

Install practices 4 and 5 will both focus on Third Down and Scoring Zone situations, as they represent the bulk of situations that must be mastered. Obviously, Third Down efficiency is a byproduct of production on 1st and 2nd down; the keys here are use of Navigation Tags to override any basic progression teaching. It is clear to see how the FALCON (Forget Advantage, Look Off to Concept) navigation tag can remove uncertainty on certain downs. To clarify, one would not want to make unilateral changes to the progression because of a Third Down situation; doing so would severely limit the explosive capability of the offense. Instead, the coaching staff is able to control when to align these thoughts with the players on the field. The play caller should be the communicator of the intent; there should be no doubt for anyone on wearing a headset or seeing a play signal as to the desire of the coaching staff (Figure 6-38). Below, with a Falcon tag, the QB's face mask will attract potentially 2 players to the post by Z, without any actual intention to throw the post. The real intent, by the play caller's tag, involves the high-low isolation all the way to secure a key conversion.

Figure 6-38. "Falcon" Navigation Tag to adjust progression

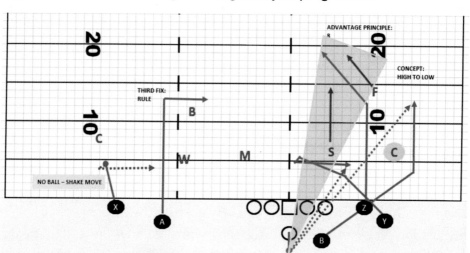

Along with Navigation Tags to re-direct thought process, there are special adaptations of route ideas specifically geared to these strategic situations. One such example is the BIKE combination tag (Figure 6-39). BIKE gets its name because of a TEN route inside of a SPEED IN; the word logic is formed: "Ten + Speed= Bike." Combined with man/press beating half field combinations, BIKE provides easy completions and run after the catch opportunities versus a variety of match-up zone techniques, making it particularly effective in both Third Down and Scoring Zone situations down to the 9- to 4- yard line.

Figure 6-39. BIKE combination.

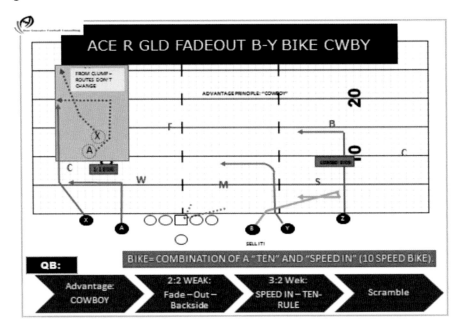

Figure 6-40. STING tag= "7 and IN & GO"

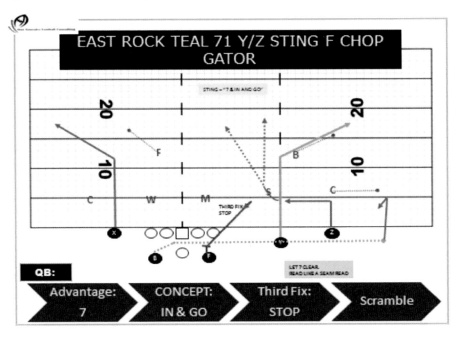

Because of the effectiveness of pattern reading, it would behoove the offense to have measures to counter popular combinations. These "move" combinations can prove to be extremely effective in the Scoring Zone; two combinations that are installed for this purpose can be the STING (Figure 6-40) and JUKE Figure (6-41) tags.

In Figure 6-41, the offense is in 2-back, 3-wide receiver personnel, inviting 2 "box" linebackers; the movement late can create a form of "match" coverage to the strength. The QB looks to X on the left as his advantage route, while the Z runs an "in and go," all the while using all the adjustment keys of a seam read. Y and B draw coverage outside, isolating the linebacker in the middle of the field. Because of the urgency of the defenders to attack familiar route combinations as the opponent gets closer to the goal line, STING can result in easy big plays. All the while, the learning of new techniques - from the QB going from advantage (7) to backside, to the receiver executing the same vertical reads learned previously – is greatly reduced.

Figure 6-41. JUKE tag= post corner.

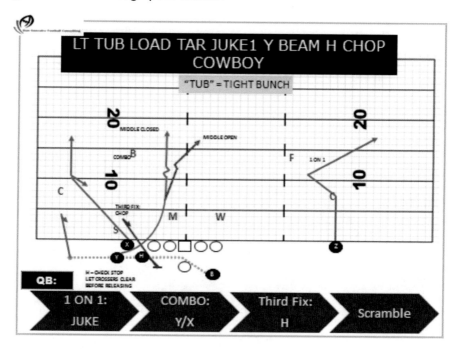

Above, the JUKE route with the COWBOY tag creates an isolated double move; the value versus a man corner is obvious. The bunch formation into the boundary can also trigger a zone adjustment – one that must have a secondary adjustment with the B's motion outside the bunch.

Should two defenders be committed to bracketing Z, as the diagram illustrates, there is an immediate stretch on the backside safety. Once again, there is no new learning on the part of the X and Y. For the quarterback, the eyes to the right, swinging back to the left to find a seam read, creates a familiar picture. The elongated stem of the X (because of the bunch alignment) gives the passer extra time to go to him should the B squeeze the seam read. TAR protection means there is a 6-man protection despite being in "empty."

One must, of course, have a plan for tighter areas of the Scoring Zone. While the different field zones in this area of the will be covered in subsequent chapters of this text, it cannot go unnoticed that much of the concentration of the fourth and fifth sections of installation are devoted to unique situations that occur as the offense nears the opposing goal line. It can become very apparent to the offense that many existing combinations have this element of flexibility (Figure 6-42).

Figure 6-42. Option route example at the +5 yard line.

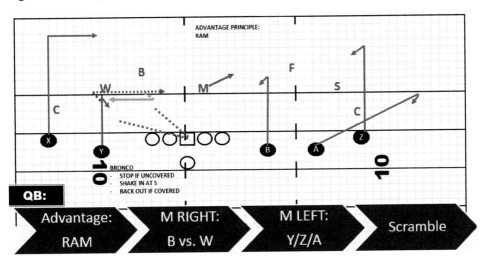

The above play is part of standard the one-word call menu, yet can have an applications in the tight Scoring Zone, as shown here. One of the key factors for its effectiveness is the reluctance of the defense to play Cover 2 in this area of the field, eliminating the squeeze from the corner, and allowing a back-line throw should the B safety and W linebacker squeeze the option route. Though this is a generic example, it does give the reader an example of the breadth across situations that many play concepts possess.

The sixth installation segment will be devoted to end of game situations, deceptive plays, and short yardage eventualities, keeping in mind that the repetition and development still has a long road ahead before being game-ready. As one can clearly see, however, all play concepts are installed very early on, and with the straightforward approach to learning for the player (understanding that this method does require a coach to be highly organized), the repetitions build upon themselves. Though the look at installation here was extremely high-level, there should be enough for the reader to glean ideas from which to model a similar method for introducing the offense.

7

Polishing the Offense: Player and System Development

Polishing the Offense: Player and System Development

Installing and practicing are two very different ideas, yet are often confused for one another. Here, the initial teaching cycle happens very rapidly, and drills, skills, culture and methodology are established. Most of practice from that point should be the refinement of situational awareness and individual techniques necessary to execute the offensive axioms that have been established. One item the late, great Homer Smith preached was the lesson that "practice time is limited; digestion time is not." In other words, the overall teaching cycle should go from individual development (Off Season), to installation of scheme (Spring and Summer practice), to scheme development (In-season Practice).

Once the offense is installed, practice time devoted to learning play assignments (outside of natural game planned adjustments), rather than the enhancement of skills and the execution of scheme, is an inefficient use of time. This is particularly true in today's age of technology, where information can be dispensed to players over a number of mediums outside of the actual practice environment. Teams that spend too much time in the installation phase often face two significant problems: 1) they inevitably don't have enough live reps in the more advanced, situational football elements of the offense, and thus 2) never live up to the potential of the physical talent available. Strictly from the standpoint of teaching the offense, in order to reach the maximum potential of a team, non-installation practices must be centered on the creation of solutions for the problems that opponents will create. Central to this premise, of course, is the development of the quarterback position within a program.

QB Development. The need for players to better themselves athletically in the off-season is without question; furthermore, there are other aspects of development (cultural, mental, and emotional toughness) that require a team environment (an off season program). At the very same time, some portion of the off-season must account for the advancement of the quarterback group, because of there is a wide array of emotional, physical, and mental aspects that must be enhanced in order to give a program outstanding quarterback play. It is no secret that elite play at the quarterback position can elevate a team's chance of success, and even surpass an overall talent disparity between teams. While there are obvious leaps a program can make with a great talent, winning play at the high school level can be developed with less than top Division 1 talent. In this system, development of the position begins as soon as early as possible; Quarterback School can be blended into strength and speed development, and covers comprehensive skills inherent to playing the position (Figure 7-1).

Figure 7-1. Aspects of QB Development

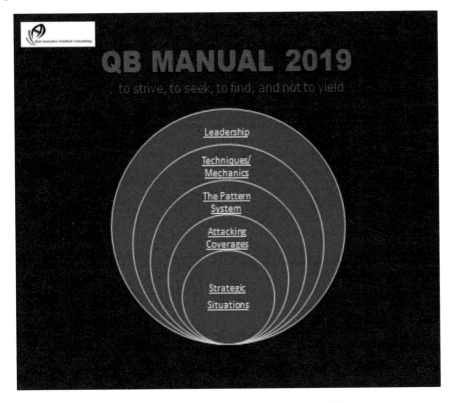

The Quarterback Manual, which is the overarching philosophical and technical thesis on the program's expectation of the position, is the (virtual) text from which the syllabus for the development program will be created. As the reader can gather from the above, every competency is covered in broad strokes (Figure 7-2), with the narrow focus to be sharpened under the watchful eye of the coaching staff.

Figure 7-2. Examples of QB Manual Slides

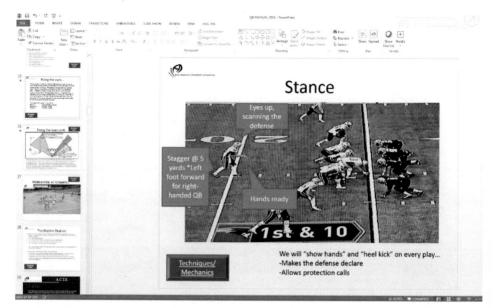

From leadership, to mechanical aspects, to the philosophy of how the offense is built, no stone is left unturned in giving each QB in the program the tools to run the team, should the opportunity present itself. Of course, not all aspects of the offense are introduced to every level; however, there are no shortcuts in terms of leadership training or the mechanical facets that are relevant.

Figure 7-3. Imbedded video example.

To keep pace with other technological advances as well as appeal to a number of learning styles, imbedded videos and animation are also present to bring more than simple drawings (Figure 7-3). In addition to the basic components of the offense, situational thinking is also covered. It is critical for the quarterback as a leader to possess a more mature understanding of the theory behind every call, as well exhibit the ability to anticipate the needs of each situation, naturally solidifying him as a "go-to" person among his peers.

Further, in-depth analysis and attack scenarios for all major coverage categories is delineated. Not only are basic coverage schemes studied, but also anticipated adjustments as well. Critical thinking in terms of how formations create alterations on the part of the defense, and how that weakens both the offense and defense, must be taught if championship-caliber production from the QB spot is to be attained in a consistent manner.

Figure 7-4. Sample coverage attack scenario

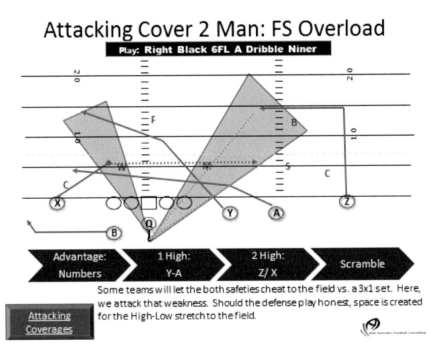

Developing the Offense. Much like developing the quarterback position, multiple aspects of the pass offense must be developed. Setting aside the obvious need to develop offensive linemen and pass protection techniques, the development of the passing game can be accelerated with common ingredients that can be ascertained at every level of a program. While the obvious desire for prototypical players always remains, most are in a situation where the cultivation of these elements is necessary.

Establishing man-to-man threats. Many passing games rely on big-bodied receivers (who are typically long-striders) to be the targets of typical quick game emphasis. However, many of these types of passing games have been derailed by physical defensive play. Throughout the section on installation, it is clear that a theme of destroying man coverage is a priority (Figures 7-5 and 7-6). In creating a practice plan, receiver priority must be given to developing the mindset of not only winning at the line of scrimmage but at the breakpoint of the route as well.

Figure 7-5. Day 1 Install Pass featuring man-beater principles.

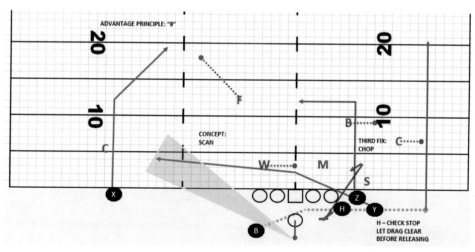

Above, there is the "banjo" coverage that is dictated by the bunch formation; the presence pre-snap of a fourth receiver will likely dislodge defenders. There is a great possibility that Y has a chance to beat W with 2/3 of the field to run to, or the B must chase through traffic.

Figure 7-6. Man to man pass example 2.

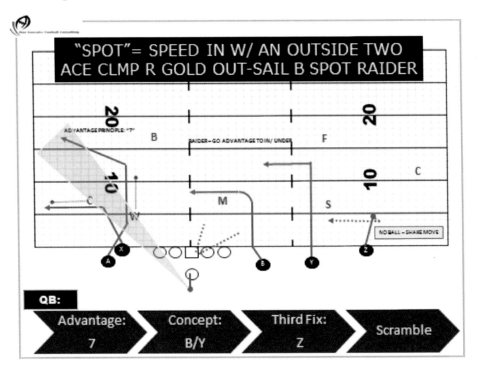

All versions of the "7" route can be considered among the best at attacking man coverage, whether using standard or stacked releases. Above, "banjo" coverage is dictated by the stack, and X's immediate outside release puts W covering the A on a sail route, basically putting him at a disadvantage from the start. Though the release is puts the receiver in good position; he must maintain his vertical position through contact, and finish with a great break.

Even "on air" or "catch drill" sessions should contain these elements, as the preparation should be to execute under the toughest of circumstances (Figure 7-7). As the drag route is a foundational route that can be found across multiple pattern structures, releases, reactions, catching, and a high volume of repetitions can all be found in a drill that can serve as an excellent warm up period.

Figure 7-7. Drag Drill

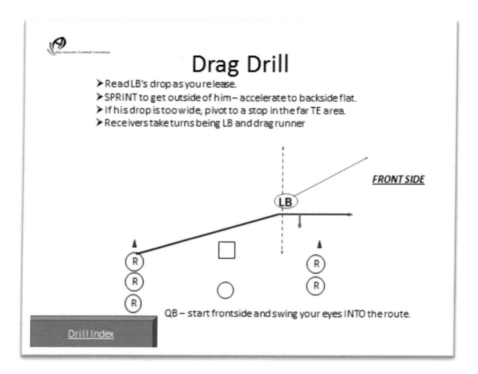

The BRONCO, 3, and TEN routes, found throughout the Installation Plan, also give a variety of high-percentage "double move" routes that present a tall order for any single coverage defender. The "3" and "TEN" (Figure 7-8) also provide a relatively inexpensive possibilities for coaches in the event that a player with a great feel for option routes fails to materialize. With the predetermined nature of both of these routes, the quarterback is never guessing on the break of the route and can thus be more decisive, leading to better RAC opportunities.

Figure 7-8. 3 (left) and TEN (right) routes; highlighted in green.

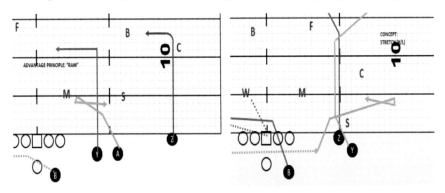

Developing a seam reader. Like the drag route, the Seam Read is a bedrock route that represents many aspects of the offense in general: aggressive, smart, and versatile. Therefore, it is taught to all position groups in order to find as many ways as possible to attack zone coverage. This is critical, as the setup of the offense is to discourage man coverage. No matter what the coverage, every practice repetition must prepare players for physical play; the integrity of landmarks must be kept, all the while maintaining focus on the availability of the seam (Figure 7-9).

Figure 7-9. Drill for coaching the Seam Read.

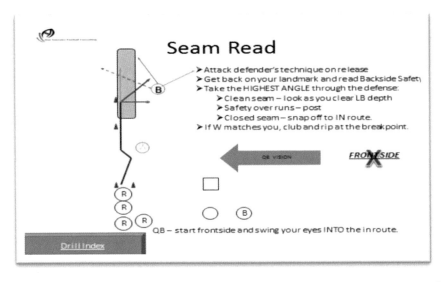

When running vertical read routes, the receiver must be FULL SPEED at his decision depth; one of the most common mistakes occurs when the route runner predetermines the decision, and raises his shoulders before the break point. The coach wants to harp on the coaching point, "anticipate, but don't predetermine." As with any route, shoulders should be forward at the decision depth, creating the illusion of depth even if the route is breaking off. And, of course, it goes without saying that the passer must maintain the rhythm of the play. His eyes should be on the frontside hash (the seam read is always on the backside hash relative to the play call), and go through the eye placement and footwork of an Advantage Route, then move his eyes and hitch to be set for the throw to the seam read. Similar to the setup of the Drag Drill, players should rotate from receiver to safety. Doing so not only provides better speed than if a coach were playing safety, but it also builds understanding as to the movements of the defender, and what those movements signify relative to the receiver's decision making process.

Developing possession receiving skills. Throughout the total offensive catalog, one can see that there are, in virtually every call, high percentage aspects at the quarterback's disposal. Completion percentages in this offense have reached the 70 percent range on multiple occasions; this level of efficiency cannot be achieved without concentrated teaching in effectively stretching zone pass defenders (Figure 7-10).

Figure 7-10. Stretch vs. flat defender

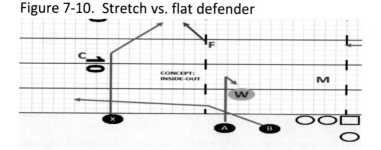

The 4 and 5 route, which are prevalent in most offenses, requires meticulous technique, as well as an understanding the effect of surrounding routes, in order to get maximum return on investment. In Diagram 7-11, using an inside 5 (Stick) route, coaching points at the top of the route can be seen.

Figure 7-11. Coaching the end of the route

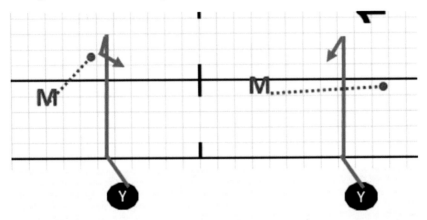

On the left, the underneath defender opens to wall the 5 route; he must hold the collision out of the break, re-trace steps, and expect the ball to the outside, if thrown. Of course, there is a good possibility the ball would go to a complimentary route in the flat, and this route would effectively seal pursuit. On the right, the underneath defender disappears underneath the route runner as he bursts up the field; the route should then take a tight inside turn, being careful not to drift into the next underneath defender.

Turn routes, such as the stick, curl, and spacing hook, should have some similar logic at the top of the stem; club or rip moves can be executed during the drill phase of individual. A simplistic method of getting all the skills necessary would be the splitting of duties within a drill (Figure 7-12).

Figure 7-12. Four Line Drill illustration.

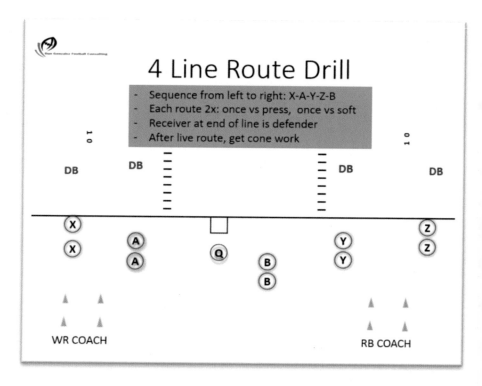

For example, the QB coach can direct a route session (with wither an LOS or breakpoint obstacle provided by another player) with QBs and WR, while the receivers coach can take another group through cone drills. Likewise, the RPO/ Screen/ QB read game can be covered in a circuit-type drill, where the read, ball handling, blocking, and screen portions can all be covered in a continuous loop. With the WR, QB, and RB groups being represented, efficient use of time can ensure maximum repetitions and that all players are getting practice within all aspects of the offense.

As one can see, in both the Advantage Route (Four Line Drill) and Half Field RPO periods, multiple skills can be covered. This type of thinking must permiate the thought process of coaches, as they sequence drills not just because of a standard in practice formats, but because they are necessary skills that must be mastered.

Figure 7-13. Sample practice grid.

TIME	X&Z	Y&A	QB	B	H-B	OL
10	DRAG DRILL					PASS SETS
15	4 LINE - ADVANTAGE ROUTES (ALT TO CATCH)					RUN Combos
	H20					
10	STALK/ SCREEN		RUN ACTIONS/READS		SPLIT ZONE	
10	1/2 FIELD RPO - ROTATE TO CONES (GOB, RIP/CLUB)				GAP	
	H20					
10	TEAM TAKEOFF - LIGHTNING, SPECIAL, SCREEN, ALERT					
20	CONCEPT/3RD FIX VS D - Seam Read, Bronco, Crooked 0, Spot, Bike, Cuff, Sail, Sting, Fort, Pump, Bengal, Fire Flame 9 and Flare					PASS SETS, RUN STEPS, BLITZ PICKUP
	H2O					
10	1 ON 1		ROTATE BETWEEN	RUN HULL/ BLITZ PICKUP		
15	PASS HULL (24 plays)					PASS RUSH
20	TEAM OFFENSE (40 plays)					
	END					

As noted previously, the majority of practice is a time for skill development. Except for introductory or installation segments (perhaps during the introduction of a weekly plan), there is no time for the teaching of assignments. If this is the case, one will always lose the battle on the practice field to the opponent. Teaching sessions can be present for review/ preview, such as the "Team Takeoff" portion ,where the full offensive unit can come together at teaching tempo prior to the normal team segment, which is at full speed. As noted in the sample practice schedule in

Figure 7-13, there is an accelerated play per minute expectation; even at the youth level, a coach was assigned to the pace of practice, where the ball was to be snapped every 30 seconds. Coaches can, and should, of course augment to the needs of the team; for example, the PASS HULL period could be a "TEAM PASS VERSUS PRESSURE" situation or a combines "9 on 9" pass session where the 7 on 7 group is accompanied by 2 pass protectores and rushers.

Figure 7-14. Applying individual practice throws to game situations.

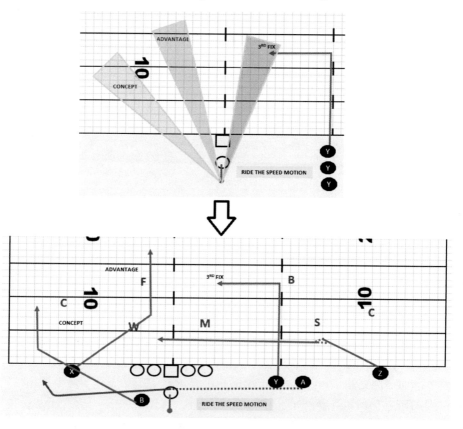

The ability to practice (and play) fast can only be made possible with the proper base being set at the onset of teaching. A set number of skills, such as the use of a rip or club technique at the breakpoint of a route, are set early on in planning sessions, just as the use of a "speed cut" or delay techniques is used to create natural separation between routes, so a pass pattern maintains the proper spacing necessary for the passer to scan from one route to another. From the perspective of maintaining the integrity of ACTS, every route thrown must be done with the timing and movement of the eyes involved (Figure 7-14).

In Figure 7-14, the top illustration shows the movements of the QB's eyes when throwing to a single route vs. no defenders. Despite the absence of opposition, the offense never executes a single maneuver without the thought of how it applies to a play as it would be run in a game. The bottom diagram shows what the total pattern would look like. Referring back to the top, the quarterback would ride an imaginary sweep fake, then put his eyes and feet to the Advantage, then Concept, then finally to the Third Fix, throwing the single route to the Y. At all times, the rhythm of each play must be considered.

Moreover, the specific adjustments of the offense can be done so that the offense carries the maximum amount of answers versus a given defense, yet maintain play economy; the following diagrams provide examples of these scenarios:

Figure 7-15. "Alert" example

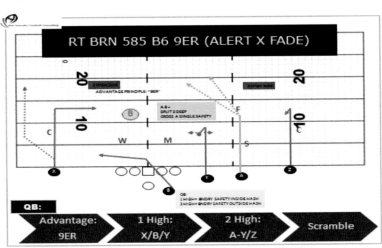

The diagram above represents many facets that are relatively basic for the offense, but create unique problems for the defense. In its basic structure, the components to defeat either 1-high or 2-high defense are present, with an "Alert" tag the QB can use if he gets a definitive 2-high look. As with all NINER tags, the disposition of the boundary safety gives the QB much information. If he rotates inside the hash, there will be a high-low stretch on the W (Figure 7-16). If, however, there is a clear Cover 2 look, the QB will call "Alert" at the line of scrimmage, taking the X off of his RULE route and now assigning him to the FADE, as designated by the play call (Figure 7-17). The effect of this adjustment cannot be understated, as it not only provides play economy, but reinforces coaching points that we teach the QB as well.

Figure 7-16. Previous play vs Single High Read.

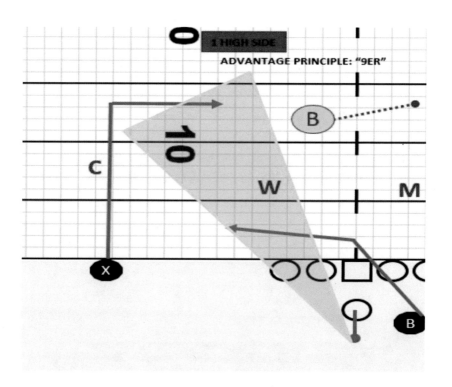

Figure 7-17. "ALERT" vs 2 High.

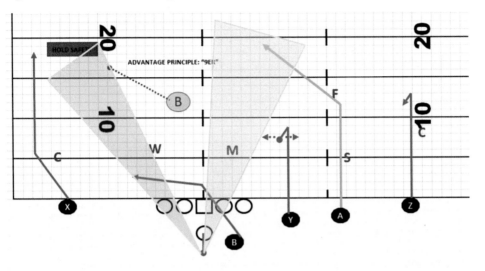

Figure 7-16 illustrates a rather elementary high low stretch that is possible with no safety involvement towards the RULE route. However, if there were no route adjustment made when the coverage (based on film study) is clearly 2-deep, there is a chance of the route by X bleeding into the frontside pattern. With the adjustment to a FADE at the command of the QB, the face mask of the passer (blue vision triangle) can keep the safety expanding off of the hash, opening space for the front side combination. The stretch on the M backer can be easily anticipated (green vision triangle), but the coaching point of starting eyes in front of every inside route can be reinforced here simply by the play call.

The smart use of "ALERT" calls makes practice more efficient, and learning more sophisticated, as waste is eliminated; another passing game example of an ALERT tag is seen in Figure 7-18.

Figure 7-18. Additional ALERT example.

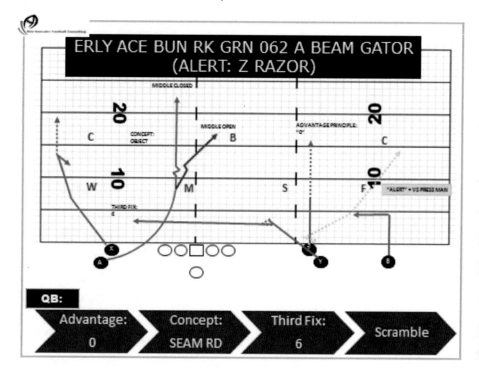

Here, with a primarily zone-beating pass pattern, the advantage route can be adjusted to a RAZOR (a term for a "tight fade"). From the split of the Z receiver in the formation, it would become almost impossible for a corner to jam and outrun the receiver to the face spot, as opposed to a fade that is executed from a regular split. From a tight alignment as is depicted in the diagram, a man defender's only option is to interfere, or guess. Because the RAZOR is even faster than a 7, the offensive coaches are giving the passer an additional tool to beat man, but at an even faster release time.

Most coaches can remember a time in run-dominated offenses where their high school coaches would have to draw up every scheme versus every anticipated front; the major drawback is the amount of practice time devoted to things that will never be encountered; a passing game such as this, with streamlined schemes for the line, counters this problem. While on the subject of efficiency, it should be pointed out that the coaching staff must take great measures to be not only understanding the system, but to use the exact same verbiage. Nothing can be more confusing to a learner that has four different coaches make the same coaching point using different words. From the junior high on up, if the coaches are to get the most out of their teaching, the exact catch phrases must be emphasized in order to "coach on the run."

This entire offense has been used successfully in team situations where participation numbers were low; despite smaller increments in some aspects of practice, time can be won back with more individualized time with fewer players. As it has been shown here, repetitions can be won in all hours of the off-season, and learning can occur in an unlimited fashion, so long as the system is set up to make sense to a player; everything done needs to be looked at from their perspective, as they are the ones that must execute.

8

Game Planning

Game Planning

Perhaps no part of coaching offensive football gets is misunderstood as game planning. This is because a vast majority of people that coach do so on a level, or in a sport, that requires very little game planning – certainly nothing compared to what happens at the varsity level in high school or above. Many have the misconception that great play calling is a matter of surprising the defense, when it is actually the product of great data-based analysis and common sense. In fact, all successful teams have strong tendencies; to simply go against tendencies with the goal of "fooling" the defense is a recipe for mediocrity. Instead, a well-designed offensive system will have components that compliment others, all the while having mental pictures and techniques remain consistent for players.

From the points made in the chapter covering installation, specific situations are addressed in this system as plays are installed.   For example, the FIT tag (Figure 8-1), standing for "Fork Inside of a 2," is specifically designed for the Scoring Zone from the +14 to the +9.

Figure 8-1. Y FIT combination from GROUP (+15 yard line).

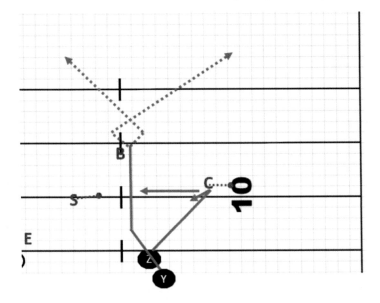

With much of the situational offense installed, the weekly routine can then become one of evaluation on two levels: personnel and scheme. A staff must come up with ways to manage mismatches in the opponent's favor; likewise, adjustments to problem defenses must come to fruition in a relatively short period of time. Once again, it becomes critical to have a system of where enough variety can be achieved, without new learning during the course of the week. The following represent major points of emphasis that should be considered by the staff when preparing for an opponent.

Data Breakdown. From the perspective of data, it is important to have definition, but to not have so many fields that the data becomes diluted. This is one area where "less is more," particularly from the formation perspective (Figure 8-2). There is only so much that can be gleaned from miniscule variations, particularly as an offensive coach studies an opponent's defense. Aside from the formation cores listed in the left column, credence is given, however, to the condensing of receiver splits or the alignment of the defense when the formation strength is into the boundary (FIB).

Figure 8-2. Breakdown Criteria

Formation Criteria	Stack/Bunch/Motion	Blitz (5, 6, or 7)	FIB (Y/N)	Situation	1st Play After
2x2					
3x1					
Empty					
2 Backs					
2 TE, 1 Back					
2 TE, 2 Back					

The last two columns become of particular interest, as it is critical for a coaching staff to detect trends in the situational calls of the opponent. Situations obviously govern many calls, as the defense will, for example, defend the line to gain, rather than play base defense; situational calls will be defined in greater detail later on in this chapter. One thing that can prove to be beneficial in the breakdown is the "1st Play After" column (Figure 8-3). People are creatures of habit, and so it is incumbent on the staff to build a list of these situations to study.

Figure 8-3. "1st Play After" criteria.

1st Play After
Opponent Score
They score
They turn over
O Big Play
O Penalty
D Penalty - Auto 1st
3rd Long Conversion

Football is a game of momentum and emotion, and that will never change; therefore, knowing how a team will respond to the ebbs and flows of a game are readily available, especially with technology that can pull these lists with a click of a mouse. A play caller can then prepare calls that are not based on down and distance, but rather the energy flow of the game. What do they come back with after a scoop and score? What happens after the QB throws a strike for a first down on 3rd and 13? What does the defensive play caller do to stem the tide when their offense commits a turnover? It is easy to become isolated in one's side of the ball; simple notation on the part of the input coach can assure that preparation leaves no stone unturned.

Of ultimate importance, it is required that coaches understand personnel, both the opponent's as well as their own. Without comprehending the limits of what the team's personnel will allow, one can become susceptible to "chasing ghosts" – spending time contemplating eventualities that will not materialize, simply because the personnel would create an unsoundness in such a tactic. A play caller's priority is to give the offensive team the highest possible percentage chance of success every snap; therefore, it stands to reason that once data is arranged in easily consumable formats, the outline of the game plan can begin to take form, starting naturally with protection.

Protection. In a passing offense, evaluating this facet of the game is always the top priority. To reiterate, protection is a shared responsibility between every position group and thus, must be evaluated in this manner. While many coaches can consider themselves aficionados of the passing game, the demise of many promising offensive performances can be attributed to the negative plays that come as a result of pressure. Schematically, there are options within the pocket passing game that scan be considered to nullify a great pass rusher, namely the CHIP technique as previously described, as well as what is referred to as AWARENESS (Figure 8-4).

Figure 8-4. AWARENESS as it pertains to pass protection.

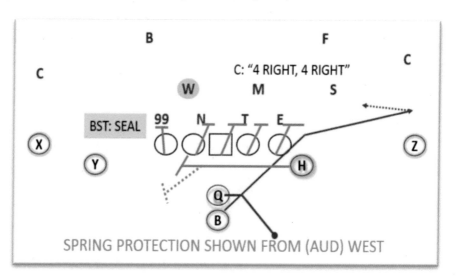

SPRING PROTECTION SHOWN FROM (AUD) WEST

To note here is that "awareness" features the free man if an assigned blitzer does not blitz. The "danger players" are identified, so players are given priority as to where their eyes will go if a blitz pick up assignment drops into coverage. Using "Stretch Pass" protection, the H is assigned to the backside W in the event of a blitz. If W drops, or flows over to the slide, H will

148

leave an impression on 99, the designated danger player. For a back to be notified of an AWARENESS assignment, the colors MAROON or METAL are given (the M stand for MAX) in dropback (Figure 8-5); the "M" stands for "MAX" – the back is a full time protector.

Figure 8-5. MAX protection example

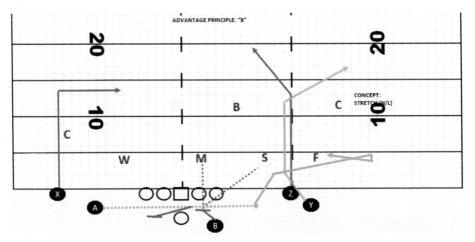

Above, a three level pattern structure called with MAROON protection; the back checks the first blitzer inside-out to his side, just as he would in BROWN protection, but then works to the danger player to help secure a more firm pocket for the QB.

The addition of extra protectors DOES NOT equate to extra time unless there is a specific target for the extra person. One particular point along this train of thought is the use of an H-Back or running back in full slide protection (Figure 8-6); though widely accepted, some less than favorable results can occur. Below, one can see how despite the classification of a "zone" protection, single blocks cannot be avoided, and the alignment of the defense puts the H-Back/ Tight End on the defensive end. In pass protection, this is clearly a poor matchup for the offense, as defensive ends are accustomed to rushing the passer, and the offensive player's time in practice is rarely associated with pass protection. Further, the defense can actually get two pass rushing mismatches, should it so choose, as the defense can align to put the end as the responsibility of the running back. Clearly, having 2 eligible receivers stay in to protect can actually hinder protections, and there is no added time for the passer, as the left guard and left tackle still have single blocks on their assignments.

Figure 8-6. Full slide Protection

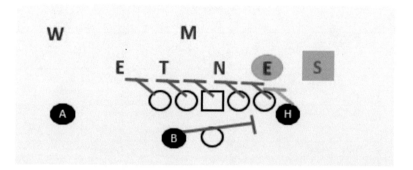

Where an H-Back body can make a difference, however, is if he is stepped off the ball, and can act like a FB, with the ability to pick have a dual pick-up (Figure 8-7). The benefit over a FB lies in the fact that a defense must account for a TE/H-Back like a tight end, and thus treat the personnel on the field like "11" personnel, rather than a 2-back grouping. The typically larger H-Back/ TE body has obvious benefits over a smaller running back as well.

Figure 8-7. H-Back as a check-releaser

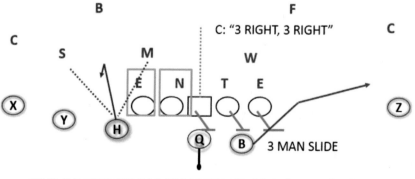

TAR PROTECTION SHOWN FROM (AUDI) EAST

Further, effective use of SLAM (chip) releases can help buy additional time. In the event of an unfavorable mismatch (or if the team has physical receivers but no true H-back), and alternative can be provided where the line slides to the 4-man side, which puts the "chipper" on a slot defender, freeing him to most likely deliver a rib shot on the defensive end before releasing (Figure 8-8). Of course, if the back is free-released, it would be desirable to have a "sort" to that side, with the right guard tackle taking the inside-most rusher between the end and W, should they both rush.

Figure 8-8. Alternative H-Back scheme.

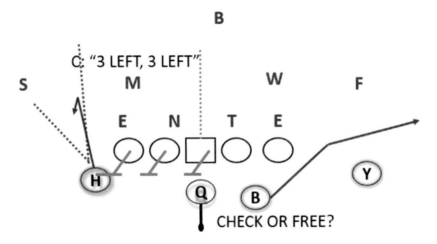

Having such flexibility is to be desired, as there are times when the offense might want to trigger a blitz in exchange for plays down the field; some of these situations will be covered later in the chapter. But because the pressure plan is a unit focus, rather than simply that of the offensive line, there are protection features that must be evaluated as part of a holistic plan. The following are examples of universal aspects that should be studied in the planning process.

The application of tempo. Offenses, in the opinion of this author, must take advantage of the ability to run plays at the fastest tempos as a means to help pass protection. In fact, it is often a focal point of the "mini scripts" that are developed when putting together the total plan (Figure 8-9). To clarify, there are not just 1-word play calls, but rather a series of high-percentage, specifically focused plays that are run with the purpose of maintaining ball control, and testing the stamina of frontal defenders.

Figure 8-9. Organized fast-rhythm plays to aid pass protection.

RUN SIT - QUICK RHYTHM - WEAR DOWN FRONT						
ACE R	18	R GLD FADE-OUT, B/Y BIKE CWBY	1	A/D L	36	L GRN FADE-OUT, B/A BIKE CWBY
ACE	37	BLUE SPLIT RT READ X NOW	2	LEFT	56	BLUE SPLIT RT READ A NOW
A ROCK	17	GRP RK GRN 039 A SLNT X2 RAM	3	DEUCE (A)	35	CLMP LD GLD 039 Y SLNT Z2 RAM
RT L	87	SWEEP RT (ALRT: NOW)	4	LT R	105	SWEEP LT (ALRT: NOW)
LT LD		LOAD GOLD X PASS Y 7	5	LT LD		LOAD GOLD X PASS Y 7
RIGHT	85	RED SEAL LT ALL STOP (ALRT RKT)	6	LEFT	103	BLUE SEAL RT ALL STOP (ALRT LSR)
	M1	MENU 1-2-3 (NOW)	7		M1	MENU 1-2-3 (NOW)
RIGHT		RENO NOW-PUMP-0 B1 HALO	8	LEFT		LINCOLN NOW-PUMP-0 B1 HALO
	LRL	LTNING RALPH	9		LLR	LTNING LARRY
	LPA	LTNING PALM	10		LFI	LTNING FIST
RT LOAD	83	L D GLD OUT 9 A2 MAV	11	LT ROCK	101	RK GRN OUT 9 A2 MAV

In order to maximize this weapon's effectiveness, it is critical to study the substitution patterns of the opposing front; this should be as known of a quantity as the front structure itself. Above, here is a sample from a call sheet from the 2018 season. The opponent's defensive line was extremely imposing; in fact, the offense's line only had graded as having just two positive matchups across the five (including the center versus ILB blitz). Because the identity of the offensive team was rooted firmly in its quarterback and skill position players, minimizing drop back pass attempts was not an option.   In studying substitution patterns, however, it was discovered that starters were left on the field without a solid plan for rotation (despite depth in the form of roster numbers). So, as part of a holistic approach to protecting the passer, it was deemed necessary to throw the ball *more*, albeit in a very quick-rhythm, high percentage manner.   In other words, the offense was going to FORCE the front to rush the passer over and over again, though in a carefully scripted manner (Figure 8-8). As drives got going, tempo would be used to prevent substitution; at that point, the more ambitious calls of the plan could then be unleashed.

Figure 8-10.   Example of a pass to aid in protection.

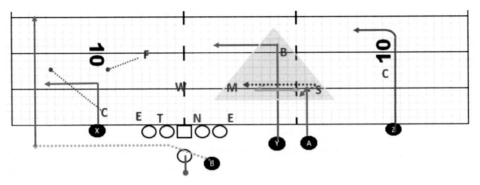

Upon surface inspection, the above pass would rarely be thought of as a "protection-centric" call; however, further scrutiny reveals several dynamics produce that exact effect.   First, the 3x1 set brought forth a "match" look of sorts, with the field corner manned up, and M, S, and B forming a triangle read over the 2 slot receivers (Y and A). This means the M must remove from the box enough to match the release of Y; as a result, W must be in an approximate position of a regular middle linebacker. These adjustments alone remove many pressure possibilities. Next, the motion of the back creates a cavity in the defense; it is unlikely that the press corner will remain. So, to the weak side, the QB has a quick-game throw, and to the frontside, something almost as quick (Figure 8-11).   If the Will is the adjuster to motion, the likely scenario is the M carrying with Y, and S being left to chase A. With this now being man coverage, it is probable that A will defeat S as he plants hand whips back to the outside. This is an easy throw and catch, and the better the S reads and breaks, the more open the receiver will be.

As the game unfolded, the plan was executed beautifully, as the ball was released at 2.0 seconds (or faster) <u>for completions</u> 16 times; along with ensuing deep shots, the result was a 38-16 rout of a bigger, stronger team.

Figure 8-11. Front side matchups.

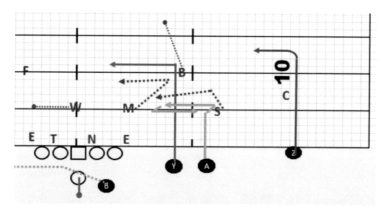

Protecting the pocket in a spread environment is critical, in that it allows the offense to attack every defensive structure, and has carryover to every strategic situation. More importantly, it allows the offense to get the ball to every eligible receiver. That being said, it is to be noted that a plan for unsound attacks on the pocket be present (Figure 8-12).

Figure 8-12. Call Sheet notation.

	SCRN	ACE		43	ROC
		RT R B SP	RIGHT	41	REN
		ACE ROCK		42	ROC
	Sprint	A BUN		44	BUN
PROTECT POCKET		RIGHT	(FLY)	45	DAF
		(OXY) RT		89	STR
		ACE		46	CLN
	PAP	ACE		47	A SF
		(O) RT L B SP		48	B SF
	QUICKS	A GRP RK		17	GRF
		ACE R		18	R G
		RIGHT		83	LD
		(O) RT R		84	R G

The illustration above shows a section of the call sheet, depicting exactly how actions are thought of here; many teams assign similar purpose to these actions. While screens and RPOs are well-documented for their ability to aid protection, the following represent a few adjustments that make these categories particularly effective:

Movement adjustments. One particularly effective tweak to sprint passes was to execute them exclusively from "Empty" sets (Figures 8-13 and 8-14). As one can surmise from the earlier chapters of this book, the ability to move the running back is a key feature of the offensive structure. By installing the sprint-out attack from empty, an offense can protect its no-back drop back concepts because interior blitzes and games can be discouraged. Because the position of the B-back in the slot is a common occurrence, this feature can aid the normal operation of the offense by limiting the pressure packages the defense can present to the offense.

Figure 8-13. Sprint example 1.

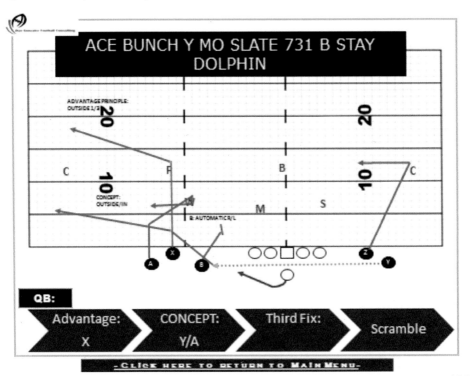

Figure 8-14. Sprint example 2.

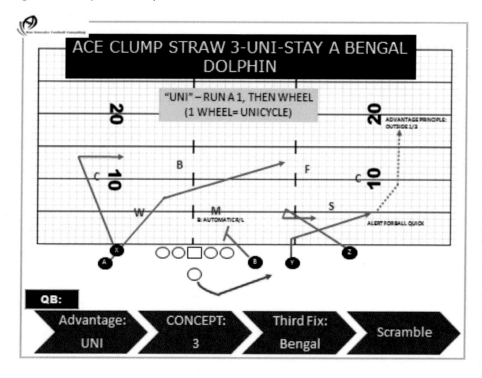

Screen/ Pass Options (SPOs). Though not a new idea at all, there are simple tweaks that have aided the effectiveness of these patterns (Figure 8-15). Here, the space for pulling linemen

Figure 8-15. Screen/Pass Option

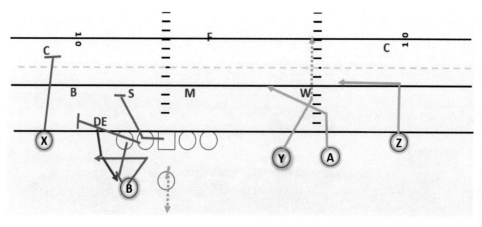

is reduced by having the screen run into the boundary, thus tightening landmarks putting the OL closer to their assignment. Then, because of a flexible system of calling frontside routes, a "man beater" of the week can be dialed up to the field. The thinking here is that a rub of a special design would be available to take in quick rhythm, then throw the boundary screen versus zone. Many already do this with "Stick" to the front side, but here there is more of a man-zone delineation – once again making things very deliberate for the quarterback.

Protection Alerts. With the prevalence of tempo in the offense, there are great opportunities to use protection ALERT tags to take advantage of a defense "selling" out to create pressure, as they must show intentions before the snap. Using one example, the illustration of how the system is geared to maximize the attack (Figure 8-16).

Figure 8-16. Call with protection ALERT.

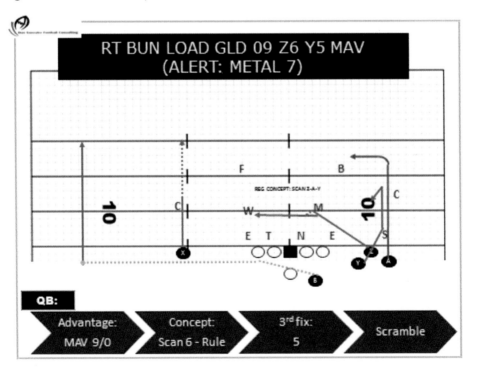

Above, there is a pass designed for the Scoring Zone, to be run around the 15-yard line. Using the Maverick advantage principle, it can be understood that the defense must communicate quickly to the motion, after needing to declare to a bunch situation to the boundary. With perfect play from the defense, there is still an excellent working route, with a double move on the M linebacker, combined with a layered route to combat a cloud adjustment. If there is a pressure alignment, the protection is changed to a MAX protection, deleting the motion, and the X's route is now a man-beating 7 route (Figure 8-17).

Figure 8-17. ALERT adjustment to previous play call.

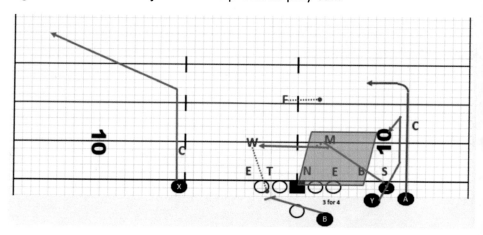

For the line, the communication received is simply "Gold;" it is GOLD protection unless the ALERT call is made – the adjustment is on the part of the back, so the ALERT is irrelevant to them. The B can be kept in to put a body on W, and the split of X for the 0 already has him in position to run his 7 route.

Coverage. The other aspect in planning the passing attack is obviously based on the back end of the defense. Much of the template is already set in the off-season, as the staff formulates a picture of not only who plays each position (Figure 8-18), but in the model for attacking opponent interpretations as well. Going beyond the Quarterback Manual's baseline version of attacking coverages, there are also several resources that coaches can go back to in the time sensitive environment of the season.

Figure 8-18. Personnel prototype

PERSONNEL PROTOTYPES:

QB- Extremely intelligent, tough, and accurate. Nimble feet and can be taught anticipation. Can make all advantage throws in rhythm. Athletic enough to break the pocket on scrambles and able to run designed QB runs is a plus, but MUST be able to throw the football. Great poise and leadership ability.

B- An all around threat. Size and/or 40-time are not important. Will attack in blitz pickup. Will follow blockers and get the cutback lane. Breaks tackles and gets the tough yard. Can line up as a WR and run routes.

Y - Our most trusted receiver, and perhaps best overall "football player." Smart enough to move around and run read routes. Great in the slot or out wide. Can run read/option type routes (Drag/ streak read/ Turn/ Option). Cannot be covered man to man. Can run speed sweeps and reverses.

X&Z- Big, physical receivers. Great hands. Able to go up for a jump ball. Great on fades, posts, curls, speed outs, digs, comebacks. Great, physical stalk and crack blocker. Good enough to force a safety to play over the top of him. Great on screens, and possession- type routes.

A- Physical receiver. The next Y, with many of the same attributes. Can attract both safeties on any deep middle route. Great on option and underneath routes. Forces bracket coverage in the slot. Can't be covered by a LB or safety (forces Dime).

H/Y (TE/H-back type) - Big and physical. Can kick out DEs, wham DTs and wrap/lead on LBers. Can reach block a DE (perhaps with the help of motion). Great hands. Always reliable as a possession receiver. Can run vertical routes. Can pick up a blitzer.

F (2ⁿᵈ RB or FB)- Many of the same characteristics as B. Attacks a LB blitz. Good hands. Breaks tackles and gets the tough yards. Can block in space.

- CLICK HERE TO RETURN TO GENERAL INFO DIRECTORY-

One such resource is something termed as HIT LISTS. Going beyond normal sets of questions that are answered in the off-season (Figure 8-19), actual weaknesses in coverage are matched with skill sets and typical patterns.   The talent level of the team determines a given weakness; for example, the wide-field flat against Cover 4 cannot be termed a weakness if the offense is unable to capitalize. Likewise, solutions are also confined by the protection constraints that are available. Rather than very general statements on the coverage, specific portions of the defense are targeted, so that a series of plays can be used. The goal here is to create a chain reaction of events (referred to in some circles as the OODA loop) that cause the pass defense to break down as adjustments by the defense are made; while some

159

of this is done pre-snap with the ability to ALERT, some of this is achieved with post-snap adjustments or Advantage Principles.

Figure 8-19. Off-season coverage breakdown format

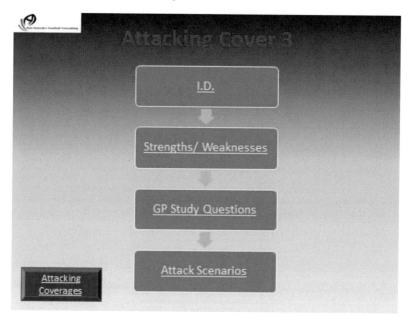

Figure 8-20 reveals a sample of the HIT LIST menu, which can serve as a guide to springboard ideas for game planning. Below, each thumbnail represents imbedded video with notes and illustration to not only teach, but to serve as a springboard for new ideas as well. With a flexible system of structuring pass combinations along with a way to direct the passer's thought process, there is a great opportunity to build attack scenarios. Once again, the process begins in the off-season, and serves as a means to create a platform for spring installation. In the actual Hit List menu shown, there are ten different ideas to attack each of three specific parts of Cover 4, resulting in 30 total methods from which to build a set of options for the game plan. Because of the structures that are well-defined, one can generate a list of ideas (referred to as a READY LIST) from which simple adjustments can be made with minimal teaching once the base is installed/ taught.

Figure 8-20.   HIT LIST menu example.

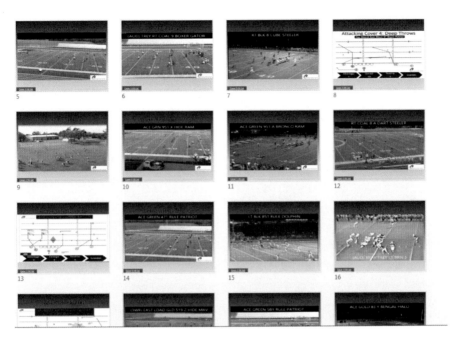

A staff can then develop a means for collecting these ideas and creating a visual catalog so the collective thought process can be organized. With all the flexibility in the system to go along with the numerous ways to generate answers, it is important to set boundaries, while at the same time, keep potential ideas on the horizon for eventual use. In terms of formulating a plan, however, the use of formation worksheets has proven useful (Figure 8-21).   While certainly not a new idea, this process definitely gives a purpose to each and every potential call in the plan; most importantly it creates synergy between the play caller, coaching staff, and quarterback.

Formation Worksheets. These worksheets give definition to the anticipated alignment to a given formation, and ensure that the coaching staff is on the same page in terms of answers to specific problems. In the world of the up-tempo offense, it is increasingly necessary to be able to check the adherence to the plan, rather than falling into the trap of calling what is familiar.

Figure 8-21. Formation worksheet for basic 3x1 Sets.

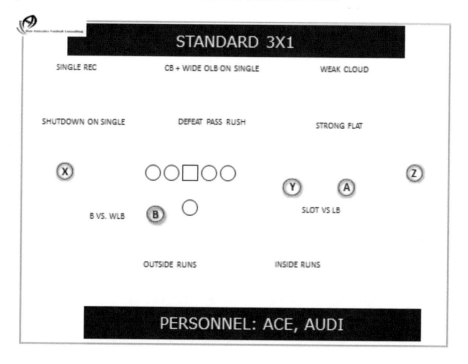

Above, one can see categories that a staff can examine relative to 3x1 sets. On the top left hand side of the chart, special note should be taken that contingencies are made for situations where the single receiver is winning his matchup and when he is not. Typically, the defense will compensate elsewhere in both scenarios, so it is important to make note. For example, a shutdown corner on a single receiver can accompany either pressure or the attempt to bracket another receiver; it is critical to have this understanding so that an adequate number of solutions are available. It should also be understood by the staff that multiple solutions are desired; simply having one or two answers might not be enough to win a tight contest. Again, the driver should always be doing what is necessary to beat top competition; while all the answers might not be needed in Week 2, they might be needed in Week 8, and certainly in Week 14. The goal is that these answers are identified, and backed by practice repetitions throughout the season, so that the players have a legitimate chance to deliver in crunch time. The answers from these worksheets should be readily available on game day, either as part of the call sheet itself or as supplemental material in the press box or on the sideline (Figure 8-22).

Figure 8-22. Worksheet section on call sheet.

ROOT FORMATION: RT/ LT								
SINGLE CAN WIN			BEAT PRESSURE			VACANT STR FLAT		
73	BDRY-89 DRG	91	75	467 X/Z 8	93		TIGER/ LION	
	PALM/ FIST		74	RUSH-SWIRL-6 BO	92	75	467 X/Z 8 9ER	93
84	SIGNAL	102	89	SPR 89SWIRL	107	79	468 SAIL B1	97
16	MO CH BRNCO	33	80	585	98	89	SPR 59CUFF	107
SHUTDOWN ON SINGLE			C3: WIDE OLB WK			SLOTS VS LB		
77	#3 TOP	95	75	467 X/Z 8	93		RALPH/LARRY	
78	SM9 A DOT	96		PALM/FIST		73	BDRY 89 DRG	91
82	BNGL BUMP	100	81	B BRONCO	99	83	09 XZ4, Y OUT	101
B VS WLB			WEAK CLOUD			16	MO BRONCO	34
78	SM9	96	79	Y BEAMER	97	1	MO DRG	19
	FIST		76	A BMR (RULE)	94	81	B BRONCO A 3	99
81	B BRONCO	99	90	9SLAM Y SPOT	108	77	9 TOP	95
4 RELEASERS STRONG			RK/ LD WK			RK/ LD STR		
84	228 B6	102	77	SEAM-9-TOP BOX	95	73	89 A DRG	91
75	468 X/Z8 B1	93	83	09 XZ4 Y OUT	101	54	JUKE	72
74	RUSH-SWRL-6 BO	92	79	76 Y BMR	97	50	STING	68

Matchups. All the data analyzed should all point to the most important aspects of coaching the game – the matchups. While many can visualize or understand this idea, it is important to truly look at this subject on multiple levels.

First, it is critical to vet and analyze fully. For instance, when facing an elite player, a coach would do a disservice to his players to simply say "this guy is committed to (major football power)" and end the conversation there. What are the weaknesses? Are there ways to neutralize the talent? Is the player a two-way player so that a combined plan with the defensive staff can be formulated? Is he a high profile recruit that will succumb to "business decisions?"

Second, matchups that fall into the favor of the offense should revert to the scheme. There are plenty of solutions in the offense, and one of the important keys becomes using the system to put the defense in the desired disadvantage. For example, in the diagram below, the defense plays a 3-down front, which makes the isolation of a RAM read less desirable. However, with the tight split of X for his "COP" (Corner- Stop) route, a cloud adjustment can be dictated. With the Y not split outside the hash, he will have leverage on the backside safety (B) on his BAR route, which basically isolates him vertically on the M linebacker. So, despite the Quarters principle call from the defensive coordinator, an inside linebacker is forced to cover deep with his help over the top removed.

Figure 8-23. Manipulation of the defense.

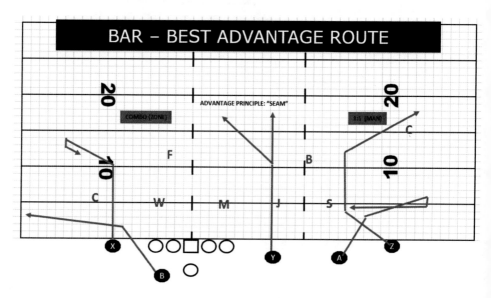

While there is clearly the need to create explosive plays, matchups in the most consistent offenses are dialed up in a high-percentage manner. Here (Figure 8-25), a 3-level structure is given a small tweak that allows for more space on the outlet receiver. The "move" on the Z's route not only facilitates an easier release across the field, but it delays the route slightly as well. As a result, M and S linebackers can wall their respective receivers, creating more room for the run after the catch. If a typical shallow is used, he would be further across the field, and the S linebacker has an opportunity to cut off the receiver before turning up.

Figure 8-25. Underneath double move.

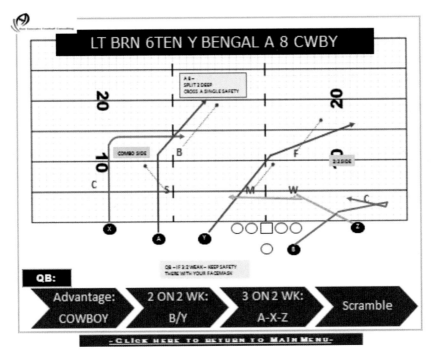

Lastly, personnel matchups need to be evaluated from a total plays perspective; coaches must know the "ceiling" for each of their own players. In other words, coaches must know the maximum number of plays a player can play before becoming a liability. Some players may provide much needed depth, but can be exposed by the opposition if left on the field past that limit. Player rotations must account for these boundaries; most teams cannot wait for games to be "in hand" before resting starters.

Time-efficient Assembly of the Plan. The above route adjustment is an example of nuance that is lost on the casual bystander, yet can make a world of difference to those within the offense. Another medium in which an immeasurable advantage can be gained lies in the aspect of time efficiency. Everything in the offense from the "X and O's" perspective is based on versatility and ease in learning; likewise, the preparation aspect is based on removing as much wasted movement as possible, so that other aspects of the game can be managed.

The primary time-saving feature of the planning system might be centered on the wristband used to call plays (Figure 8-26). As detailed previously, this is a fool-proof method of communicating the play to the players on the field, without losing time with elaborate signals; further, it allows for a system where the flexibility is maximized because of minimal rote memorization involved in learning. Moreover, the efficiency added to the planning process is unmatched.

Figure 8-26. View of wristband/game plan populator.

K4	▼	:	✕ ✓ f_x	='Wrist Cards'!G25								

	A	B	C	Q	R	S	T	U	V
1									
2	Periods	Weekly	Situation						
3	Practiced	Reps	RUNS	H	Per	Formation	Alt Align	WB	Play
4	RH, T	10	Foundation Run 1 w Att	R		ACE		55	RED SPLIT LT READ Z NOW
5	RH, T	12	Foundation Run 1a w Mo	R		LEFT		56	BLUE SPLIT RT READ A NOW
6	RH, T	12	Foundation Run 2 w Att	R		RT TUB		57	RED SEAL LT Y LOB
7	RH, T	12	Foundation Run 3			LEFT	© RT TUB	58	RED Q SPLIT RT FLASH LT
8	RH, T	10	Adj Run 1 (RPO)			LEFT		103	BLUE SEAL RT ALL STOP (ALRT LSR)
9	T	2	Adj Run 2 (RPO)	R	*WEST*	WEST A FLM		104	A FLAME BLUE SPLIT RT RD A FLARE
10	T	6	Opp Run 1	R		LT R B SP	D CL L Y SP	105	SWEEP LT (ALRT: NOW)
11	T	6	Opp Run 2	R		LT		106	CK- RED QB SWP RT CRK X NOW
12	T	4	Screen 1	R		LEFT	(L R SP)	59	LINCOLN X NOW AY FOLD -7 RAZOR

The first means by which the band system aids the offensive staff is the manner in which it forces the coaches to LIMIT play calls, thus eliminating inefficient practice routines. There is a limited amount of practice time, so the manner in which one can perform at an optimum level is to have reps built out over time with the utilization of a system of consistent structures.

Next, as the wristband form is filled out, the play names populate to a virtual "Game Plan Board." The coach can alter or add formation or personnel information, and then fill in each situational section by simply typing in the wristband number (Figure 8-27). Time is saved and the opportunity for error is lessened, as the whole call does not need to be re-entered.

Figure 8-27. Wristband numbers populate to situational script

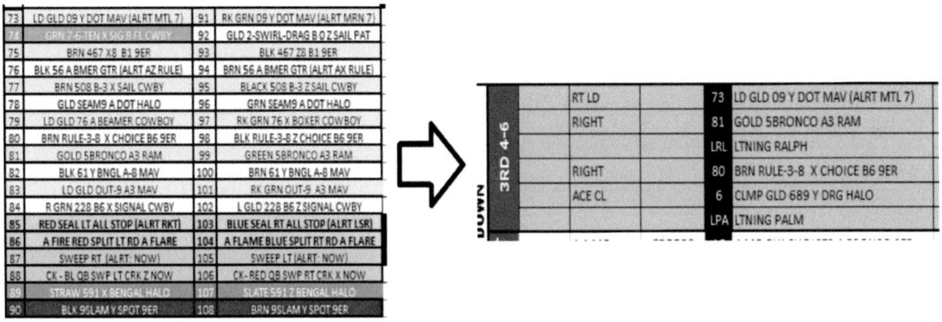

73	LD GLD 09 Y DOT MAV (ALRT MTL 7)	91	RK GRN 09 Y DOT MAV (ALRT MRN 7)
74	GRN 7-6-TEN X SIG 9 FL CWBY	92	GLD 2-SWIRL-DRAG B 0 Z SAIL PAT
75	BRN 467 X8 B1 9ER	93	BLK 467 Z8 B1 9ER
76	BLK 56 A BMER GTR (ALRT AZ RULE)	94	BRN 56 A BMER GTR (ALRT AX RULE)
77	BRN 508 B-3 X SAIL CWBY	95	BLACK 508 B-3 Z SAIL CWBY
78	GLD SEAM9 A DOT HALO	96	GRN SEAM9 A DOT HALO
79	LD GLD 76 A BEAMER COWBOY	97	RK GRN 76 X BOXER COWBOY
80	BRN RULE-3-8 X CHOICE B6 9ER	98	BLK RULE-3-8 Z CHOICE B6 9ER
81	GOLD 5BRONCO A3 RAM	99	GREEN 5BRONCO A3 RAM
82	BLK 61 Y BNGL A-8 MAV	100	BRN 61 Y BNGL A-8 MAV
83	LD GLD OUT-9 A3 MAV	101	RK GRN OUT-9 A3 MAV
84	R GRN 228 B6 X SIGNAL CWBY	102	L GLD 228 B6 Z SIGNAL CWBY
85	RED SEAL LT ALL STOP (ALRT RKT)	103	BLUE SEAL RT ALL STOP (ALRT LSR)
86	A FIRE RED SPLIT LT RD A FLARE	104	A FLAME BLUE SPLIT RT RD A FLARE
87	SWEEP RT (ALRT: NOW)	105	SWEEP LT (ALRT: NOW)
88	CK - BL QB SWP LT CRK Z NOW	106	CK - RED QB SWP RT CRK X NOW
89	STRAW 591 X BENGAL HALO	107	SLATE 591 Z BENGAL HALO
90	BLK 9SLAM Y SPOT 9ER	108	BRN 9SLAM Y SPOT 9ER

3RD 4-6		RT LD		73	LD GLD 09 Y DOT MAV (ALRT MTL 7)
		RIGHT		81	GOLD 5BRONCO A3 RAM
				LRL	LTNING RALPH
		RIGHT		80	BRN RULE-3-8 X CHOICE B6 9ER
		ACE CL		6	CLMP GLD 689 Y DRG HALO
				LPA	LTNING PALM

Above, the play card on the left mirrors that which is worn by the player; as band numbers are entered into the situational script, the play name automatically populates. As an example, on the top right, the number 73 was entered and the following appears in the right hand column: "LD GLD 09 Y DOT MAV (ALRT MTL 7)." As these calls are entered into the Game Plan Board, they simultaneously fill out the call sheet for the game.

While these features in and of themselves are impressive, the greatest time-saving benefit comes as the Game Plan entries automatically fill out the practice scripts for each day. Because each section that is scripted is tied to a game situation, any given call can see up multiple looks; the staff simply inputs, and the script will populate accordingly (Figure 8-28). It is no stretch to estimate that a process such as this can save the offensive staff eight to ten hours of preparation time.

Figure 8-28. Game board play and defensive input.

			Practice 1	Practice 2	Practice 3*
WB	Play	TAGS	Run Sit D	3rd Dn D	SZ D
33	L GLD 200 Y BRONCO RAM		43 C2	NI OV C1	42 OV C4

Across multiple points of checks and balances, the offensive staff is held accountable to ensure that every call has a purpose and has been executed in practice. Along with these best practices, the elimination of the need to script allows the staff more time to study the opponent, and prepare their own team for dealing with the pressure filled calls that will win or lose ball games.

Situational Calls. An additional benefit of having a system requiring minimal new learning is the additional effort that can be devoted to situational football. Below is a table listing of situations for data breakdown that is consistent with the game planning process.

Figure 8-29. Situational summary.

Situations
Run Sit (1st or 2nd DN)
Pass Sit (1st >10, 2nd >7)
Short Yardage (3rd or 4th 1-3)
3rd & Med (4-6)
3rd Long (7-12)
3rd X Long (13+)
Backed up
SZ 25-14 (1st/2nd)
SZ 13-10 (1st/2nd)
SZ 25-14 (1st/2nd)
SZ 9-5 (1st/2nd)
SZ +4
SZ 3rd or 4th Down
Two Minute Drive
2-PT Attempt

Likewise, practice plans are aligned with the situations of the day; Scoring Zone days, for instance, might have dedicated Blitz Pickup sessions due to the frequency of pressure from a given defensive team. While most of these situations are pretty typical, the system setup and QB development process here adds an extra layer of not only understanding, but versatility in already common techniques as well.

Figure 8-30. Excerpt from Quarterback Manual.

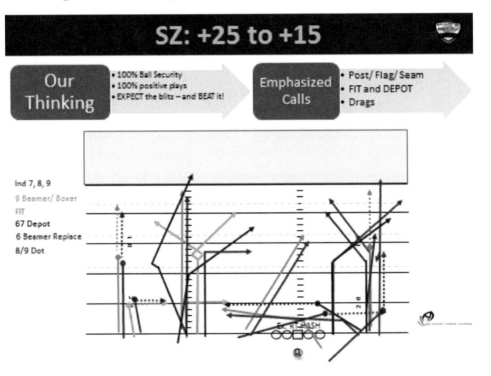

Situational teaching starts in QB School in the spring (Figure 8-31), building a foundation that is easy to expand upon, not only from an X's and O's perspective, but in the development of specific skills as well. For example, one Key Performance Indicator (KPI) for Scoring Zone efficiency is Touchdowns/Attempt. In order to meet Championship Level performance here of 1 touchdown: 4 attempts, completions must come with yardage, increasing the importance of the 7 route. Thus, reliable production from 7 routes is a critical factor for efficiency. This is among the many reasons for the prominence of 7 route combinations during the installation phase of teaching; the pattern shown here (Figure 8-31) illustrates the planning/ thinking that is driven by tangible achievement levels in a given situation.

Figure 8-31. Scoring Zone application of existing ideas.

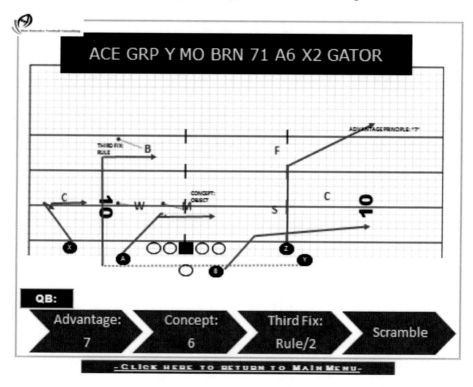

The above not only utilizes an outside receiver on a familiar "smash"-type read, but it isolates the A on a horizontal space route as well. The stack alignment creates predictable indicators, and the motion creates movement that will isolate and define the backside outlets. All the while, condensed field area is considered, as lateral space is valued by carefully plotting timing aspects so that receivers are not invading the same space at the same time, negating their effect.

One particular category in the Scoring Zone that is perhaps slightly different than others relates to Third Downs in that territory (Figure 8-32). To be determined on an individual basis is whether or not 3rd Downs are truly possession downs – at what point on the field is the offense in 4-down territory where 3rd down might be a means to set up a manageable 4th down attempt? This thinking can obviously change once the flow of the game unfolds; once again, it is beneficial to have Navigation Tags as a means of guiding the passer's thinking on a down-by-down basis.

Figure 8-32. Sample section of Scoring Zone Third Downs

3RD DN 10-4								
(O) RT	77	BRN 508 B-3 X SAIL CWBY		1	(O) LT	95	BLACK 508 B-3 Z SAIL CWBY	
A GRP Y MO	2	GRP Y MO BRN 71 A6 X2 GATOR		2	A CL A MO	20	CLMP A MO BLK 71 Y6 Z2 GATOR	
RT LD	83	LD GLD OUT-9 A3 MAV	*A31*	3	(O) LT RK	101	RK GRN OUT-9 A3 MAV	*A13*

The goal here is to have pre-existing plays in the plan that can flow into these situations, always with the thought that they are familiar to the offense, and can be enhanced by overriding the read tag or by having an ALERT attached.

Open Field Third Downs are approached with more detail than simply throwing for the sticks. For example, thoughts are included for the "3rd and Medium" script for a particular game below:

Figure 8-33. Third & 4-6 notes.

3rd DOWN
3rd 4-6 1 (NO pressure)
3rd 4-6 2 (NO pressure)
3rd 4-6 3 (Pot. Explosive)
3rd 4-6 4 (Pot. Explosive)
3rd 4-6 5 (Look Alike)
3rd 4-6 6 (Look Alike)

In preparing six calls for this scenario, it was found important that no matter what, the possibility of a sack early on was unacceptable. Whatever momentum the defense would be allowed to have, a pressure on the quarterback would not be part of the equation. Whether the scripted call is a quick pass, screen, or a drop back with an easy receiver release made possible by formation or motion (Figure 8-34), the offense will play the next down with the confidence that the protection plan will be solid throughout the game.

Figure 8-34. DASH pass to negate pressure.

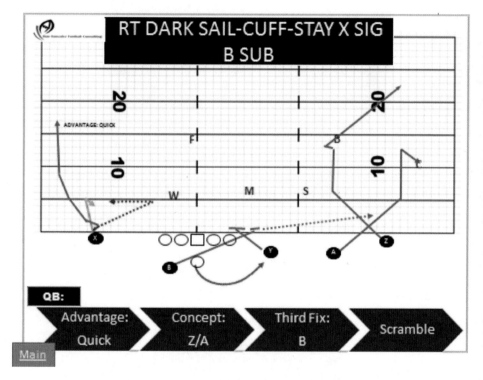

The "Dash" action above combines a backside quick pattern that can be thrown vs 1 on 1 coverage with a sprint pass to the field. The blending of these ideas results in a situation where much of protection should be solid. Though the overall pattern has limitations because only the outside thirds of the field are threatened, one can have confidence that the interior is fortified versus the pass rush.

While the first two 3rd and MED calls are focused on quick rhythm/ protection, the next two have the element of creating a possible explosive play in mind. The example in Figure 8-35 reveals possible thinking for such a situation. Combining both TRAIL and RUB components to garner a completion, there is the additional explosive play to the back versus a blitz or low –playing M linebacker in split-safety coverages. It is important to have such ideas, as 3rd Down is typically thought of as a time where the defense will try to force the narrative; this propensity should be taken advantage of.

Figure 8-35. Potential explosive play for 3rd and Medium.

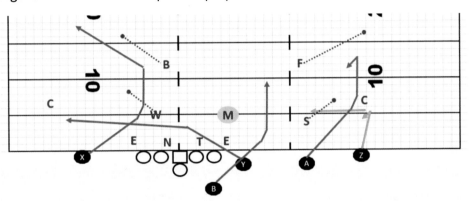

Finally, the last two calls are scripted for plays that are closely resemble other key ideas in the game plan. As these plays are at the end of the prepared calls, the logic applies that they could present themselves later in the game, where possessions are limited. Depending on the situation, the acute need to convert might be present; the offense can level the playing field by playing off of reactions during the ball game. Of course, careful planning and extreme organization is a must.

Attack Ideas/ Mini Scripts. Much has been made of the scripting of openers as it pertains to play calling; while there are certainly elements that can benefit the offense, the ebb and flow of a game is often too volatile at the high school level. While there are certainly exceptions due to superior talent or elite individual performers, the ability to go from top to bottom of a planned script rarely presents itself.   Instead, what is presented here is a twist on the idea of the 25-play opening script (Figure 8-36). The staff selects the primary keys to defeating the opposing defense, and from there, creates "mini scripts" based on each premise.

Figure 8-36. Mini script section of the call sheet.

		RUN SIT - QUICK RHYTHM - WEAR DOWN FRONT				
ACE R	18	R GLD FADE-OUT, B/Y BIKE CWBY	1	A/DL	36	L GRN FADE-OUT, B/A BIKE CWBY
ACE	37	BLUE SPLIT RT READ X NOW	4	LEFT	56	BLUE SPLIT RT READ A NOW
A ROCK	17	GRP RK GRN 039 A SLNT X2 RAM	3	DEUCE (A)	35	CLMP LD GLD 039 Y SLNT Z2 RAM
RT L	87	SWEEP RT (ALRT: NOW)	2	LT R	105	SWEEP LT (ALRT: NOW)
LT LD		LOAD GOLD X PASS Y 7	5	LT LD		LOAD GOLD X PASS Y 7
RIGHT	85	RED SEAL LT ALL STOP (ALRT RKT)	6	LEFT	103	BLUE SEAL RT ALL STOP (ALRT LSR)
	M1	MENU 1-2-3 (NOW)	7		M1	MENU 1-2-3 (NOW)
RIGHT		RENO NOW-PUMP-0 B1 HALO	8	LEFT		LINCOLN NOW-PUMP-0 B1 HALO
	LRL	LTNING RALPH	9		LLR	LTNING LARRY
	LPA	LTNING PALM	10		LFI	LTNING FIST
RT LOAD	83	LD GLD OUT-9 A3 MAV	11	LT ROCK	101	RK GRN OUT-9 A3 MAV
RIGHT		DARK SAIL-CUFF-STAY X SIGNAL CWBY	12	LEFT		SCARLET BOLT-TOP-STAY Z BENGAL
RT R	84	R GRN 228 B6 X SIGNAL CWBY	13	LT L	102	L GLD 228 B6 Z SIGNAL CWBY
OX RT L CBRA	76	BLK 56 A BMER GTR (ALRT AZ RULE)	14	OX LT R CBRA	94	BRN 56 A BMER GTR (ALRT AX RULE)
ACE RK	42	ROCK GRN B NOW Y LEAD XA FADEOUT	15	ACE LD	60	LD GLD B NOW A LEAD YZ FADEOUT
OXY RT	77	BRN 508 B-3 X SAIL CWBY	16	OXY LT	95	BLACK 508 B-3 Z SAIL CWBY
LEFT	106	CK-RED QB SWP RT CRK X NOW	17	RIGHT	88	CK - BL QB SWP LT CRK Z NOW
		"APEX/ BOZO"				
A A MO (BZO)	16	A MO BLK CHOICE3 A BRONCO 9ER	1	A Y MO (APX)	34	Y MO BRN CHOICE3 Y BRONCO 9ER
RT (BZO)	90	BLK 9SLAM Y SPOT 9ER	2	LT (APX)	108	BRN 9SLAM Y SPOT 9ER
RT LD (BZO)	83	LD GLD OUT-9 A3 MAV	3	LT RK (APX)	101	RK GRN OUT-9 A3 MAV
		VACANT FLAT/ UNCOVERED #3				
ACE R	18	R GLD FADE-OUT, B/Y BIKE CWBY	1	ACE L	36	L GRN FADE-OUT, B/A BIKE CWBY
RIGHT	41	RENO Z NOW AY FOLD-X RAZOR	2	LEFT	59	LINCOLN X NOW AY FOLD -Z RAZOR
ACE R	3	GRN 851 SW A TEN DOLPHIN	3	ACE L	21	GOLD 851 SW Y TEN DOLPHIN
RIGHT	89	STRAW 591 X BENGAL HALO	4	LEFT	107	SLATE 591 Z BENGAL HALO
RT L *CBRA*	76	BLK 56 A BMER GTR (ALRT AZ RULE)	5	LT R *CBRA*	94	BRN 56 A BMER GTR (ALRT AX RULE)
RIGHT	80	BRN RULE-3-8 X CHOICE B6 9ER	6	LEFT	98	BLK RULE-3-8 Z CHOICE B6 9ER
	LBR	LTNING BRONCO	7		LLR	LTNING LARRY
		FIELD= 7/ FADE/ 9				
A GR A MO	8	GRP A MO BROWN 731 B6 DOL	1	D CL Y MO	26	CLMP Y MO BLACK 731 B6 DOL
ACE	28	BRN 671 A BEAM GATR(ALRT:AX RULE)	2	ACE	10	BLK 671 Y BEAM GATR (ALRT: YZ RULE)
A GR Y MO	2	GRP Y MO BRN 71 A6 X2 GATOR	3	A CL A MO	20	CLMP A MO BLK 71 Y6 Z2 GATOR
A GRP RK	14	GRP RK GRN 672 SW A OUT COBRA	4	A CLMP LD	32	CLMP LD GLD 672 SW Y OUT COBRA
	LBN	LTNING BRN	5		LBK	LTNING BLK
ACE	13	BRN FADE-TOP-6 X BOX GATOR	6	ACE	31	BLK FADE-TOP-6 Y BEAM GATOR
		BOUNDARY= 8/ SEAM READ/ BRONCO				
LEFT	95	BLACK 508 B-3 Z SAIL CWBY	1	RIGHT	77	BRN 508 B-3 X SAIL CWBY
ACE CL R	15	R GRN 200 A BRONCO RAM	2	D GR L	33	L GLD 200 Y BRONCO RAM
ACE	4	BRN 506 X BOX GATR (ALRT: SWIRL)	3	RT TUB RK	70	RK TEAL JUKE1 A BEAM Y CHOP CWBY
	LBK	LTNING BLK	4	ACE	28	BRN 671 A BEAM GATR(ALRT:AX RULE)
A CL Y MO	25	CLMP Y MO BLK 8-SAIL-TEN B6 HLO	5	A GRP A MO	7	GRP A MO BRN 8-SAIL-TEN B6 HALO

The above example can give food for thought with this idea; it not only ensures that every call in the plan has a purpose, but it clarifies the thought process of the play caller as well. Moreover, it can assure that specific parts of the game plan that are specifically geared to the opponent are utilized; with today's trend of calling plays as rapidly as possible, it is easy for a play caller to forget the best parts of the plan. Here, the focus can be easily re-directed, and still ensure that the most critical needs of the offense are at the forefront of the play caller's mind.

The above section reveals how an offensive group might organize thoughts in regard to Open Field, Run Situation offense; similar plans are organized for critical situations as well as "1st Play After" situations as outlined in the beginning of this chapter. All the while, the system's learnability and ability to guide the passer's eye discipline on a play-by-play basis looms as a key differentiator over other systems.

9
Conclusion

Conclusion

We truly live in an age where the means to teach the passing game is more prevalent than ever before, as All 22 video, coaching clinics, and playbooks are available for public consumption. The availability of knowledge is a wonderful thing; however, it can easily be misconstrued that the understanding of football strategy and the ability to teach and execute tactically are synonymous. This is not the case! Anyone can memorize a playbook they found online or spout off the name of a play run by one's favorite professional team; it is an entirely different thing to create a foundation for teaching that allows for one's players to execute on the field. It has been this author's mission for the last two decades to synthesize beauty of the passing game, while finding the most advantageous methods for teaching to players.

One of the primary missions of the off-season is to examine different applications of ideas, and examine assimilation to the current methods (Figure 9-1). In order to do so, a complete system, rather than simply a collection of plays, is strongly recommended.

Figure 9-1. Example of Research and Development pattern.

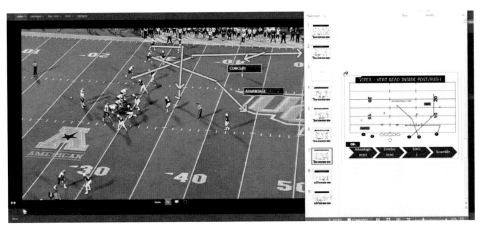

The flexibility of a system, and the ability to absorb different ideas into pre-existing structures and processes, all lead to the ability of the offense to continually evolve. Continuous improvement, without the need to discard previous teaching or repetitions, is the key in developing a successful program that will remain consistent over a sustained period of time. Here, a blueprint has been presented to give coaches ideas that would aid in the creation of such a system, from system requirements and verbiage to game planning ideas, but most of all – with the development and coaching of the quarterback in mind.

Many say that the game is cyclical and the pendulum will swing the other way; however, the state of the game, with player safety and rules favoring the passing game, say otherwise. Best of all, the ideas for attaining this on-field success are well established; the key is organizing a system that allows for teams with practice and time constraints to be more efficient than their opponents. A complete passing structure is critical in this type of situation, and this text will hopefully give the reader food for thought along those lines – creating a culture on offense where an assembly line of passers can simply "Read and Shoot."

APPENDIX 1: TERMINOLOGY GLOSSARY

NUMBERS FOR ROUTES

0   LOCKED SEAM; tight alignment.
1   FLAT by inside receiver, STOP by outside (end up in same spot).
2   UNDER - QUICK IN by inside man, STOP FIRST if by outside man.
3   PIVOT (fake drag).
4   SPACING HOOK.
5   TURN.
6   MOVE DRAG. Run a 4, then a 2 (4+2 equals 6).
7   FLAG. Tight alignment.
8   POST.
9   OUTSIDE VERTICAL. WHEEL by inside man, STUTTER GO by outside man
TEN   TRAIL. 45 degree release for 4 steps, push to the flat for 6 steps, then break back in.

INDIVIDUAL NAMED ROUTES:

FADE – TRADITIONAL QUICK GAME FADE.
JUKE – POST-FLAG. 5 STEPS VERTICAL, 3 STEPS TO POST, THEN DROP HIPS AND BREAK TO SIDELINE.
OUT – 5 YARD OUT.
RAZOR – TIGHT FADE – SPLIT NO MORE THAN 4 INSIDE #S IN BOUNDARY AND HASH TO THE FIELD.
SAIL – "7 AFTER INSIDE LEVERAGE;" JUST A NORMAL 7 ROUTE WITH AN INSIDE RELEASE TO GET TO THE BREAKPOINT
SEAM – LOCKED SEAM BY WR FROM WIDE ALIGNMENT. SWITCH RELEASE, THEN UP THE HASH

SHAKE – FAKE PIVOT TO TAGGED RECEIVER
SLANT – TRADITIONAL 3- STEP SLANT

TAG TERMS:

ALERT – some plays have adjustments built in to the call. If qb says "alert" – run that adjustment

BEAM – seam read by tagged inside receiver; outside receiver runs a "read 5". Beam is code for "backside seam"

BEAMER – CODE FOR "BEAM WITH AN EXTRA RECEIVER" BECAUSE WE ARE RUNNING TO TRIPS– Y WILL RUN A "CROOKED ZERO"

BENGAL – "BACKSIDE ANGLE," WHICH IS A DEEP CROSSING ROUTE

BIKE – A COMBINATION WITH A "TEN" AND A "SPEED IN." TEN+SPEED= BIKE. SO ON B/Y BIKE, B RUNS TEN AND Y RUNS SPEED; IN Y/A SPEED, Y RUNS TEN AND A RUNS SPEED

BOSS – 6 STEP SPEED CUT OUT.

BOX – SEAM READ TO OUTSIDE RECIEIVER, AFTER PATHS SWITCH, FORMING AN "X"…INSIDE RECEIVER WILL RUN A READ 9.

BOXER – "BOX WITH AN EXTRA RECEIVER"

BRONCO – TAGGED RECEIVER RUNS OPTION ROUTE. IF OPEN – STOP AT 5. IF NOT, BREAK IN AT 5 AND PIVOT LIKE A 3.

BUMP – "BACKSIDE UP AND MIDDLE" – INSIDE MAN CLEARS AND OUTSIDE MAN RUNS A RULE UNDERNEATH HIM.

CHOP – "CHECK-STOP"

CHOICE – OUTSIDE RECEIVER SPRINTS TO DESIGNATED DECISION DEPTH (10 YDS FOR HIGH SCHOOL). IF HE CAN WIN DEEP – WIN! IF NOT, SNAP OFF A COMEBACK IN THE 14 YARD RANGE. MUST BE FULL SPEED AT DECISION DEPTH.

CUFF – "COMEBACK W/ UNDERNEATH 4." INSIDE RECEIVER SCREENS FOR OUTSIDE MAN RUNNING A 4 ON HIS WAY TO AN OUTSIDE COMEBACK.

DEPOT – "DOUBLE POST"

DOT – "DRAG WITH AN OUTSIDE 2;" TAGGED MAN RUNS DRAG, X OR Z TO THAT SIDE RUNS A "2"

DRAG – TAGGED MAN RUNS A DRAG; RULE FOR EVERYONE ELSE ON THAT SIDE.

DRIBBLE – "DRAG WITH AN INSIDE BENGAL"

FIST – "FLAT INSIDE A SLANT" – TAG THE FLAT RUNNER

FIT – FORK INSIDE A "2". FORK IS A POST/FLAG OPTION ROUTE. HINT OPPOSITE YOUR BREAK. ALWAYS GO TO FLAG VS. 1 HIGH.

FORT – "4 TAKEOFF"

HOOK – A DEEP 4 AT 10 YARDS OVER THE BALL

NOD – A DOUBLE MOVE ROUTE FAKING A 1, THEN TURNING UP THE SEAM

POKER – POST AND CORNER

RULE – BACKSIDE INS ALWAYS RUN IF WE AREN'T TAGGED TO DO ANYTHING.

RUSH – "RUB UNDER SWITCH" THIS IS A 3 STEP IN BY OUTSIDE RECEIVER. COME UNDER THE OUTSIDE MAN.

SCRAPE – "SWITCH CURL AND POST." OUTSIDE MAN RUNS SWITCH-CURL, AND THE INSIDE MAN RUNS SWITCH-POST

SIGNAL – QB WILL SIGNAL YOUR ROUTE AT THE LINE OF SCRIMMAGE (EX. 220 X SIGNAL)

SLAM/ SUB – FLAT ROUTE TECHNIQUES USED IN NAKED/ BOOT. SLAM – BLOCK DE 2 COUNTS. SUB – FAKE A SPLIT ZONE BLOCK AND SLIP OUT INTO THE BACKSIDE FLAT.

SPOT – "SPEED IN WITH AN OUTSIDE 2." TAGGED MAN RUNS SPEED IN; X/Z TO THAT SIDE RUNS A "2"

SPLASH – SPOT SWITCH

STING – "7 & IN-AND-GO." INSIDE MAN RUNS 7. OUTSIDE MAN RUNS A RUSH, THEN TURN UP (DOUBLE MOVE)

SWIRL – "SWITCH CURLS"

SWITCH – BASIC CHANGE UP TO RULE. TWO BACKSIDE INS, EXCEPT THE RECEIVERS SWITCH RELEASES.

SWAG – "SWITCH AND GO" – SWITCH TAKEOFF TO THE OUTSIDE RECEIVER.

TOP – "10-YARD OPTION." RUN OUT ALL THE WAY UNLESS LB DISAPPEARS UNDENEATH YOU.

TURBO – "3-RECEIVER BRONCO;" BENGAL INSIDE THE TAGGED BRONCO RUNNER

SABER – "7 AND BRONCO"...SINGLE RECEIVER IN A TIGHT SPLIT OR ATTACHED RUNS A 7 INSTEAD OF A RULE.

UNI – TAGGED RECEIVER RUNS A 1, THEN WHEELS. ONE WHEEL-UNICYLCE= "UNI"

WHIP – "WHO IS PRESSED?"   QB DESIGNATES WHO WE ARE PICKING FOR

READ TAGS

SCAN – QB HAS MULTIPLE CROSSERS COMING INTO HIS VISION
- STEELER

STRETCH READS – WE HAVE A 2 ON 1
- PATRIOT – THINK INSIDE-OUT. "I" COMES BEFORE "O."
- HALO – HIGH TO LOW.
- DOLPHIN – THINK OUTSIDE-IN. "O" COMES BEFORE "I."

OBJECT READS – OUR RECEIVER WILL BEAT ANY 1 ON 1 BECAUSE OF HIS ROUTE OPTIONS OR DOUBLE MOVE
- GATOR – GO ADVANTAGE, THEN OBJECT READ

ADVANTAGE PRINCIPLES – DISSECT THE DEFENSE FOR THE QB
- RAM – READ AWAY FROM MIKE
- 9ER – NUMBER OF SAFETIES DETERMINES SIDE. SINGLE HIGH= SINGLE RECEIVER. 2 HIGH= 2- (OR 3-) RECEIVER SIDE
- MAVERICK – MOVEMENT ADJUST VERTICAL OR REGULAR CONCEPT
- COWBOY --   "COMBO OR 1:1"

NAVIGATION TAGS: TELL THE QB A SPECIAL THOUGHT PROCESS
- COBRA – "COME OFF TO BEST RUNNER AVAILABLE. " HAVE GAME PLANNED PASSES – ADVANTAGE TO BEST RAC GUY
- FALCON – "FORGET ADVANTAGE; LOOK OFF TO CONCEPT"
- RAIDER – "READ ADVANTAGE TO BACKSIDE IN/UNDER"
- TEXAN – TOUCHDOWN TO CHECK-DOWN – WE WANT AN EXPLOSIVE
- SPIDER: SHORT-DEEP-RUN …FOR USE W NAKED GAME OR SHORT YARDAGE PAP

APPENDIX 2:
OFFENSIVE QUALITY CONTROL STANDARDS

Offensive Quality Control

Each season, 65 different criteria are systematically checked against a predetermined Reasonable/ Outstanding/ Championship performance objective.

- Championship – identified as that level of achievement necessary to be a championship contender in any conference
- Outstanding – a level of achievement that puts our performance in the upper echelon among our contenders
- Reasonable – a standard that might we logically be expected to achieve by design or concentrated effort, and us usually superior to past performance.

Our "PERFORMANCE vs. BLITZ" is also checked each week on both run and pass plays, along with our percentage of offensive error based on 5 areas of emphasis (Penalties, Drops, Fumbles Lost, Sacks, Int).

- Runs
    - Runs of 4+ vs. 0/ negative yardage runs
    - Explosives
    - Penalties
- Passes
    - Complete vs. Incomplete
    - Scrambles vs. Sacks
    - Explosives
    - Penalties

We also keep track of offensive penalties, and the strategic situations in which they occur.

We analyze SCORING ZONE performance and create a drive chart to analyze how we utilized the opportunities we had with the football.

- Attempts
- TD
- FG
- MFG
- INT
- Fumbles
- Sacks
- 4th Down Stops
- Penalties

Note: Big plays

- Six 10-yard plus runs/ game normally puts us at 150+ yards/ game rushing
- Six 18-yard plus passes/ game normally puts us at 300+ yards/ game passing
- Big plays are normally the difference in a 400+ yard offensive performance and the field position to score 28 or more points in a game.
- Normally, 450 yards per game and 34 points per game would result in a top 10 performance, regardless of league.

Quality Control Categories:

Game Plan	Championship	Outstanding	Reasonable
1. # of Runs in GP	14	15	16
2. # of Passes in GP	50	46	40
3. % Movement	35	30	25

Ball Possession	Championship	Outstanding	Reasonable
4. 7+ plays or score	50%	46%	44%
5. Fumbles lost (season)	8	9	10
6. Interceptions/Attempt	1/40	1/38	1/36
7. Penalties (season)	40	42	44
8. Holding (season)	9	11	14
9. Drive stopping penalties (season)	8	9	10
10. All 3rd downs	50%	46%	42%

Rushing Game			
11. Rush yards/ attempt	5.5	5.2	4.7
12. 1st&10 4+yards	55%	51%	47%
13. 1st & 10 rush avg. (no GL)	5.2	5.0	4.8
14. All rush 4+ yards	52%	50%	48%
15. Short Yardage Efficiency (3rd,4th<2)	85%	83%	80%
16. % 0 or – yardage runs	12%	13%	14%
17. Pass Situation Run Avg.	5.5	5.2	5.0
18. Rushing TD (Season)	22	20	18
19. Deceptives Yards/ Carry	6.5	5.8	5.5

Passing Game			
20. Yards/ Attempt (include screens)	8.5	8.0	7.5
21. Pass Completion % (include screens)	70%	67%	64%
22. Dropped Pass %	8%	9%	10%
23. Screen Avg/ Attempt	9.0	8.0	7.0

Run Situation Passes			
24. Efficiency all Run Sit Passes	62%	60%	58%
25. Eff. All 1st/10 (no screens)	58%	57%	55%
26. 1st/10 4+yards (w/ screens)	60%	59%	58%
27. 1st/10 Play Action 4+ yard	63%	61%	59%
28. All 1st/10 Drop back 4+ yards	60%	58%	56%
29. Efficiency % 2nd/1-5	62%	60%	58%
30. Efficiency %2nd/ 6-9	60%	58%	56%
31. Efficiency % Pocket Play Action	58%	57%	55%
32. Efficiency % Quick Game	80%	78%	74%

Pass Situation Passes

33. Efficiency % Pass Sit Passes	50%	48%	46%
34. Make ½ yardage 2nd/10+	45%	43%	41%
35. Efficiency % 3rd/3-5	70%	65%	60%
36. Efficiency% 3rd/6-12	50%	45%	40%
37. Efficiency% 3rd/13-17	25%	23%	20%
38. Efficiency% 3rd/18+	15%	13%	10%
39. Screen avg. per comp	10	9	8

Scoring Zone

40. TD Passes/ Attempt	1:4	1:5	1:6
41. Completion %	64%	62%	60%
42. Points per game	34	31	28
43. % TDs from +5	87%	84%	80%
44. Score (TD or FG)	80%	77%	75%
45. % TD	67%	65%	63%

Two Minute

46. % Score in 2 Minute Offense	42%	40%	38%
47. Pass comp% in 2 Minute	65%	63%	61%

QB Sacks

48. Total Sacks	1/32	1/29	1/26
49. Run Situation Sacks	1/35	1/33	1/31
50. 1/10 Sacks	1/40	1/37	1/35
51. Play Action Sacks	1/50	1/45	1/40
52. Pass Situation Sacks	1/25	1/21	1/17
53. Scoring Zone Sacks	1/28	1/26	1/24
54. Two Minute Sacks	1/33	1/32	1/30
55. Sacks on Deceptive	0	1/40	1/32

Scramble

56. Run Sit Eff. %	60%	58%	56%
57. Pass Sit Eff. %	54%	52%	50%
58. Scoring Zone Eff. %	50%	48%	46%
59. 2 Minute Eff. %	65%	63%	60%
60. SY Eff. %	100%	97%	95%

Special Calls

61. 3rd and 3-5 Run % Eff.	60%	54%	45%
62. 3rd 1-2 Pass Eff. %	100%	95%	90%
63. 2 Minute Runs Eff. %	65%	63%	60%

Big Plays/Game

64.	Runs (10 or more yards)	6	5.5	5
65.	Passes (18 or more yards)	6	5.5	5

Made in the USA
Middletown, DE
30 August 2023

37671535R00106